Undeniable Destiny

Linda Caster

Undeniable Destiny
Revised Edition

Undeniable Destiny, Copyright 2002 by Linda Caster
Undeniable Destiny, Revised Edition,
    Copyright 2004 by Linda Caster
All rights reserved

Published by Purpose Press in the USA
First printing—August, 2002
Second printing—April, 2003
Revised Edition—August, 2004

Purpose Press
PO Box 681882
Franklin, TN 37067

Cover and layout by Andrecca Design
2901 Hollis Dr Corinth, TX 76210-2295

ISBN 0-9721373-2-7

All Scripture quotations are from the New American Standard Bible, Copyright 1960, 1962, 1963, 1968, 1971, 1972, 1973, 1975, 1977, 1995 by the Lockman Foundation. Used by permission. (www. Lockman.org)

All emphasis in Scripture quotations is the author's addition.

Table of Contents

Acknowledgements

Thank you Chad, Hannah, and Grace, my three gifts straight from the heart of God. You all are a constant source of joy in my life.

Thank you mom for being the greatest. You laid the foundation years ago for me to be the person I am today.

Thank you Don and Lydia Herndon for your steadfast love and support. You've been my armor-bearers more times than I can remember. Thanks for your faithfulness and your friendship.

Thanks to all the rest of my family who have blessed me in countless ways.

Throughout the years, God has put people in my life who have been a tremendous source of strength. I need to mention some by name because they've been there through thick and thin and have always been willing to drop whatever they were doing when I've called with prayer needs. Thank you Don and Lydia, Peter and Anita Robutka, Greg and Candy Ross, Bill and Meg Greenman, Colin and Lynette Ruttle, Don and Ruth Rousu, Wes Tullis, and George Reninger. I appreciate all of you for your honesty, loyalty, and constructive criticism.

Thank you Bill Greenman for all the help on this book. You were a wealth of information and kept me on track.

Thank you MannaRelief staff, past and present. This ministry could not have gotten to where it is without your hard work.

Thanks to all of you who have prayed for me throughout the years, many of whom I've never met. I always appreciate your e-mails and letters of encouragement. May God bless you abundantly.

Last, but certainly not least, I want to thank my wonderful husband, Sam. All the challenges we've gone through have only strengthened our love. By example, you've shown me the heart of a true servant. You're undoubtedly one of the most selfless and thoughtful people I know and I'm thankful God put you in my life.

Foreword

When Linda first told me she felt inspired to write a book about our amazing journey, all I could think of was what a great testimony it would be to share with others. As I began to read the opening chapters I was overwhelmed by the years of anguish and grief she suffered because she would not turn loose of God's calling on her life.

As a "self-made" success, I had always relied on my natural instincts to guide my every business move. Then at a point when the void in my life could no longer be filled with my successes or worldly possessions, Linda prayed that God would use us for a cause greater than ourselves. We prayed that God would reveal a strategy for using my God-given talents for His glory. It's been said to be careful what you pray, because God will answer you in a way that you might not be prepared for.

In our case, that's exactly what happened. God began to reveal a miraculous calling on our lives for a business that would impact people all over the world. The problem was that He revealed the plan through Linda, who did not have one ounce of business experience.

The Bible says that God's ways are not our ways and that He will confound the wise. This story is a living testimony to those claims. For those of you who have a tendency to believe it is man's wisdom that will conquer all earthly challenges, this book will provide you with a different perspective. Luckily, you will get the message in the short time it takes to read the book. For me it took years of one disastrous experience after another to get to a point where I could yield my own instincts long enough to truly hear God's plan being revealed though the least likely person I could imagine.

It's a miracle that Linda persevered through the trying years, but I know that her testimony will be a witness to those of you who live with the frustration of not getting through to your hard-headed spouses.

While this story incorporates the intriguing elements of an exploding global business that was built around a breakthrough discovery in health, the real story is the love that God has for each of us, the grace He has to stick with us even when our pride rejects His blessings, and the reality of His presence in our day to day lives.

Sam Caster

Introduction

For some of you, this story is going to challenge many of your beliefs. It did mine. As a new Christian, I knew nothing of spiritual gifts or how God could work so dramatically in our day-to-day lives. But at a very low point in my life I turned to God and prayed that He would use me in any way He desired. God's answer to that simple, fervent prayer is the basis for the miraculous story in this book.

This is a story of how my unyielding desire to serve God strained my marriage, challenged my faith, broke my heart, caused me to feel ostracized, and put me in a situation where I begged God to release me from His call on my life. But through all the pain, frustration, and heartache came the most astounding blessings. This is a true life story of the struggle between good and evil, played out by worldly experts in an arena of high stakes business.

I am a home school mom who has never run a business or worked in a ministry. Yet God chose to reveal a plan through me which would help birth a unique company. That new company would bring to market a scientific health discovery that would generate close to a billion dollars of revenue in its first eight years. And from that company a ministry would come which would impact the lives of medically fragile children on every continent on earth.

This unlikely merging of scientific discovery, explosive business growth, and God's calling, would illicit every imaginable type of human response in the lives of all involved. From the temptations of power and greed to the reverence of humility and gratitude, from the ridicule of those paralyzed by conventional wisdom to the praise of those who would faithfully answer to a higher calling, all hearts were exposed.

Being the messenger in the midst of these enormous conflicts was not a position of choice, but of obedience. I was at odds with my husband and other business experts over issues I knew nothing about logically, only spiritually. At first it was frustrating, but thankfully my husband tried to listen, we both began to learn, and the business grew. Then, as more outsiders entered the company, it's entire direction began to shift away from God's purpose. And finally, just when it appeared that everything we'd been blessed with was in jeopardy of being completely lost, God showed up in a miraculous way that inspired the naming of this book, Undeniable Destiny.

It's my prayer that through this amazing and true story, your hearts will open to a clearer understanding of the power of prayer and the unlimited potential that God has placed in you.

To my Lord and Savior, Jesus Christ, in whom I have my being.
May this book bring honor and glory to Your Name.

Chapter One

The Journey Begins

It was June 1987, when I became a Christian. Sam and I had been married about fourteen years, and our marriage was unraveling. From the time we were first married in 1973, Sam had been successful in all of his business ventures. Not only had he been a musician and owned and managed restaurants he also founded and built one of the largest solar energy companies in the country. This led him to his next multi-million-dollar venture, his first network marketing company called Eagle Shield.

Of all his businesses it was Eagle Shield that achieved the fastest and most profitable growth. Between its founding in 1986 and its peak in 1988, the company grew to sales exceeding ten million dollars a month. In the eyes of the world, Sam was truly a self-made success story. He had accomplished so much in the arena of business that people often said he had the Midas touch.

I was a flight attendant at the time for a major airline, and we took full advantage of the benefits that come with being an airline employee. We traveled the world, and with our newfound wealth, there were no limitations to our jet-set lives. From outward appearances we lived the perfect life—the American dream—but behind closed doors it was a different story. Sam and I were moving in different directions.

Brooke Arrives

My brother, Billy, had a serious drug problem for quite a number of years. He sold as well as used drugs. Billy had custody of his daughter, Brooke, and from the time she was born, I absolutely adored her. Because of his addictive lifestyle, Billy was unable to care for Brooke, so Sam and I intervened. We both felt that it was in her best interest to live with us, and in 1987 we took her in as our own daughter.

Our lives were drastically altered. We'd had years of coming and going as we pleased, and now we had to think about not only our lives, but also the life of an eight-year-old girl. All of a sudden we were parents dealing with school, outside activities, and schedules. There were adjustments on all fronts. Schedules were new to Brooke too, but we put our all into it and made the best out of a challenging situation.

I was actually amazed at how easily we slipped into our new routine. Having a child in our home was such a blessing. Through Brooke, the Lord slowly began to teach me selflessness and patience. I began to focus on her needs and desires and less on my own. God used Brooke to show me the truly important things in life and to understand the significance of pouring out my love into someone else. In return Brooke brought a lot of joy into our home.

The problems that Sam and I had in our marriage were totally unrelated to Brooke's living with us. In retrospect, I feel the Lord actually used her to help save our marriage. There were times for both of us when we wanted to throw in the towel. But we also wanted to protect Brooke from any more heartache in her life and so we were determined not to let our problems affect her. I tried to carry on with my life as normally as possible but at times it was very difficult. I'm so thankful that I had my family and friends to help me through it.

My sister Lydia Herndon and her husband, Don, had been praying for Sam and me for a number of years. I can remember all the debates we had with them about the Bible and how narrow-minded we thought they were. We thought Don and Lydia were prejudiced towards those who didn't believe the way they did. Sam and I both were especially offended when they told us that Jesus Christ was the only way to eternal salvation. I remember them saying, "What we're telling you isn't something we're making up. It's scriptural." In John 14:6 Jesus says, *"I am the Way, the Truth, and the Life; no one comes to the Father but through Me."*

They gave us many other scriptures, which showed the way to eternal life, but we simply couldn't understand how they could possibly believe that! There were so many other faiths and religions in the world that we couldn't fathom how they could discount them all. We wanted nothing to do with a religion like Christianity that was so intolerant.

What Sam and I failed to understand was that Don and Lydia weren't giving us their opinion of Christianity. They were quoting the infallible Word of God. Their faith was based on the Truth of the Bible and nothing else. Thankfully, Don and Lydia were never "preachy" or self-righteous with us. They let us voice our opinions, but they also challenged our beliefs or lack of them. They realized that Sam and I were going to have to discover for ourselves the truth of who Christ is.

The most compelling thing we saw in them was a consistent faithfulness to their belief. They were a gentle, quiet witness to us. Don and Lydia, through their prayers for us, laid the foundation and planted the seeds in our hearts to work out our own salvation. Through those seeds God was preparing our hearts for what was ahead.

The Beginning of the Beginning

I was finally coming to the end of my rope. My marriage was slipping away, and it seemed there was nothing I could do to save it. I had known Sam since I was seventeen years old, and he was the only man I had ever loved. I couldn't imagine my life without him; yet here I was, in a situation that was out of my control. I was in a place of hopelessness.

Sam was traveling a lot more, and we had less and less to share with each other. Brooke and I spent a lot of time at Don and Lydia's house because I felt a sense of peace there. They and some of my close friends tried to comfort me, but they couldn't ease my pain. What I didn't realize was that my hopelessness went a lot deeper than my marital problems.

One night when I was alone, I thought of the conversations about Jesus that I'd had with Don and Lydia. I thought about their unwavering faith and about the peace in their lives. In the midst of those thoughts, I remembered a tragic incident that had happened years ago.

Don was in his pickup truck, backing out of the driveway, when he accidentally ran over his three-year-old son, Nick. I was in complete hysteria as I drove to meet them at the hospital. When I got there, I was astounded at the peace that was so obvious in Don and Lydia. Instead of my comforting them, they were comforting me!

I asked them how Nick was, and they said they didn't know yet, because as soon as they arrived at the emergency room, the doctors swept Nick away. I was dumfounded at their demeanor. I asked them how they could be so calm, and Don told me that on the way to the hospital, the Lord had said to him, "Don, do you trust Me no matter what? No matter what the outcome, do you really trust in Me?" Don said that he felt a peace he had never felt before, and he felt such love coming from God that he said, "Yes, Lord, I trust you no matter what."

The prognosis from the doctors was bleak. They said that because Nick was so small and the truck weighed so much, he would probably have extensive internal problems. Don and Lydia prayed and remained hopeful. Amazingly, after only three days, Nick was released from the hospital without so much as bruise. The doctors and nurses were as bewildered as I was. They said they had never witnessed anything like this before.

Remembering that incident made such an impact on me that I thought, "Maybe there's something to what they've said. Maybe

4

there's more to life than just my understanding of it." So, through my tears and my childlike words I asked, "Are you really out there God? Are You who they say You are? If so, I need you now." I cannot say that anything earth shattering happened, but I actually did feel a profound sense of peace, and I slept better that night than I had in quite some time.

Sam had been out of town, and when he got home, I shared my experience with him. I told him that from the time I'd said that prayer, I felt very peaceful. He was anything but elated. He thought I was going a little overboard, and he didn't want any part of this Christian stuff. I didn't blame him. I could not give him a tangible reason for the change in me; I didn't have a logical explanation. I just knew that, without a doubt, a transformation had taken place deep within me.

Lydia invited me to go to a Ladies' Bible study with her. I felt somewhat intimidated because I didn't know anything about the Bible, but I was willing to do anything to change my circumstances. I met a group of women who were very caring and nonjudgmental. Although I was the new Christian in the group, I felt they all accepted me.

I was surprised to learn the truth about the Bible stories that I had so ignorantly argued against in the past. I was awestruck at how, from beginning to end, the Bible fit together perfectly, like a puzzle. I came to understand that God loved me and accepted me just the way I was. He didn't ask me to change a thing about myself. But the more I read the Word, the more my faith grew, and the more I wanted to change.

Prayers That Avail Much

I began praying a lot, and it seemed that whenever I opened the Bible, I was led to exactly the answer or encouragement that I needed. I could not believe how easy this Christian life was! I just asked God for an answer, and there it would be. My faith was soaring, and I didn't doubt for a minute God's ability to do anything.

With our marriage still on the rocks, I suggested going to a Christian counselor, and Sam reluctantly went with me. It didn't last long, though, because Sam was offended by all the references to the scriptures. He thought the counselor was too condemning. I tried to be open with Sam and talk to him about my beliefs, but he just was not ready for the Truth. I told him that the reason neither of us understood the Bible was because we'd never read it. I encouraged him to do so, but to no avail. The more I talked to him or prayed for him, the more he pulled away. But, the more he pulled away, the more I drew closer to the Lord.

Somehow, I knew there was power in prayer, so I had the women in my Bible study group pray for Sam. Then I asked my friends and family to pray for him. I watched Christian television and called their prayer counselors to pray for him. Pretty soon I had Sam on virtually every prayer chain I could find.

Although we lived in Dallas, we had an apartment in California because Sam was starting a co-generation company there. Sam took this opportunity to spend as much time away from home as possible. We weren't officially separated, but we were spending more time apart than together. Sam wasn't sure if he even wanted to be married any more.

I prayed fervently for our marriage. I remember one night praying, "Lord, I'm really trying to hold on here and to be optimistic, but I need something substantial from You. I need to know that things will somehow work out between Sam and me." Five minutes later the phone rang. It was Sam! I had not talked to him in several days, and he "coincidentally" chose this time to call me. He told me that he really loved me, but he felt empty. He wanted more out of life, but he wasn't sure what "more" meant. He just needed some time alone to think things out. I told him that I would pray for him, and we hung up. I was so excited! I had asked God for a sign of hope, a reason to hang on, and He gave me one. That phone call greatly increased my faith in the power of prayer.

Shortly after that incident I was praying, and I "heard" the voice of the Lord in a way I had never heard before. Although it was not an audible voice, to me it was just as loud. God told me to stop praying for my marriage and start praying for my lost husband. Sam's spiritual life was crumbling right before my very eyes, but I was only concerned about my marriage. That day God changed my way of thinking and praying. He imparted to me a burden to pray for the needs of others and sensitivity for the hurting world around me.

During this same time, my brother was going through some of his most challenging times. God was doing everything to get his attention. Billy now not only had Don and Lydia praying for him, but also he had me praying for him as well. I had never heard the term "spiritual warfare" before, but I had just begun reading a novel by Frank Peretti entitled This Present Darkness. That book, more than anything at that time, helped me to understand what "spiritual warfare" and "spiritual darkness" were all about.

I looked for scriptures in the Bible on the subject and was amazed at how many I found. In Ephesians 6:12, God states, *"For our struggle is not against flesh and blood, but against the rulers, against the powers, against the world forces of this darkness, against spiritual forces of wickedness in the heavenly places."* The Bible also explains that the things we can't see are more real than the things we can see. The reality of those words hit me like a ton of bricks. I plainly saw that although we live in a realm that is tangible, a world that we can see, we also live in a spiritual world that we cannot see. I knew then that Sam and Billy were going through similar situations. They were coming to the end of themselves. There was literally a "war" in the heavens for their souls, but, ultimately, the choice they made would be up to them.

I understood, because of my own experiences, that it does not matter where you are in the scheme of life, a successful business-man like Sam or a drug dealer like Billy. If you don't have the Lord in your life, you're incomplete. You can buy or do things that will temporarily satisfy you or will fill a void in your life, but one day those things will no longer be enough. So I began to pray that they both would feel empty in their very souls. I prayed that they would be miserable in their misdirected quest for happiness and that noth-ing of this world would quench their desires.

It did not take long for the Lord to answer my prayers. Billy ended up in a rehab center, which he later admitted saved his life. He had literally cried out to the Lord, and his life was changed forever. God put him on a new path, a path that would put him in the midst of kids who were just like he had been, addicted to drugs and alcohol to numb their pain. Billy was able to talk to these young people in a way that no one had been able to before. Not all of them changed, but many of them did.

Billy's life was being transformed before my very eyes. He met some men who were great mentors for him. It's not that his life was easy. He still, at times, struggled with his past, but he was definitely a changed person. He ended up going to a Bible college in Florida and eventually to Liberty University in Lynchburg, Virginia. God blessed him with a wonderful wife, a precious son, and a restored relationship with his daughter, Brooke. The Lord has certainly renewed his life.

Sam's life also changed. About two months after I began pray-ing for Sam, he called me from California and told me how miser-able he was. I was ecstatic inside, knowing that God had answered my prayers. He said that the night before, he had prayed and said, "Jesus, if you're real, then lift this burden from me." Sam said that he literally felt a weight lift from him, and he knew that God had heard him. When Sam gives his testimony, he says, "Most people have to reach bottom before they call out to the Lord. I had to reach the top. I had everything that should have made my life complete—money, success, acceptance from peers and a wife who loved me—but none of that was enough."

Sam wanted to do whatever it took to get our lives back on track, so he came home and we began counseling. It wasn't easy, and at times there was quite a bit of tension, but we took things a day at a time. We found a church that we felt comfortable with. We met a group of wonderful people there who encouraged us and allowed us to grow at our own pace.

It's A Boy!

By now, we had been married for 16 years, and we decided that it was time to have children. Through our church we met a couple who had just adopted a child. We talked at length with them and decided to use the same agency that they had used. We began our home study, which actually was a catharsis for us. We both had to write our life stories and submit them, along with an infinite amount of information, to the agency.

About nine months after we were accepted, we adopted our first child. Chad Lee Caster was absolutely the apple of our eye. Sam and I could not believe that we had waited so long to adopt a baby. Brooke was the proud "big sister," and we felt more blessed than we could ever have imagined. I remember one day holding Chad in my arms, and I felt so much love for him that I began to cry. I believe that God wanted me to have an understanding of the depth of His love for me. In that moment, I was overwhelmed with an indescribable joy and gratitude for all God had done in my life.

Through prayer I had seen miracles occur in both Sam's and Billy's lives. Our marriage had been restored, and we had been blessed with Brooke and Chad. My faith was growing by leaps and bounds, and I wanted more. I prayed that God would give me a new boldness in my faith and use me for His purposes. There's an old adage that says, "Be careful what you pray for because it might just happen." I had no idea how God was about to answer my prayer. My newfound life could have stayed just as it was from that day forward, and I would have lived happily ever after, but God had a different plan for Sam and me. What God has done from that time until now will astonish you, encourage you, and bless you. Here is where the story changes from "Isn't that sweet?" to "That's unbelievable!"

Chapter Two

Trouble In Paradise

Our lives could not have been going better. We were blessed in our home and in our business. Sam even commented on how wonderful life had become through our willingness to serve God. We were new Christians... and so naive. God let us bask in this state of bliss for about six months, and then the roof started to cave in.

Sam's company, Eagle Shield, had been very successful in bringing the new technology of radiant barrier to market. Developed by the space industry, radiant barrier was like insulation in its application but much more effective. People were reporting tremendous results with their energy savings, so much so that Sam received a letter from the state Attorney General's office stating that Eagle Shield was making unsubstantiated energy claims. Their charge was that Sam had no independent, third party scientific evidence outside of the consumers' actual reported savings. They did not ask Sam to stop selling the product; they just wanted him to represent savings less than those actually being seen. Sam's immediate reaction was "We have to give in to what they want. You cannot fight the government."

This was where that boldness I had prayed for began to kick in. I felt such a deep peace and an assurance of God's hand on us. I had read a scripture in Isaiah 54:17, which has since become one that I live by: *"No weapon that is formed against you will prosper; and every tongue that accuses you in judgment you will condemn."* Since we had done nothing wrong, I felt we had to take a stand for what was right. By now my faith was so strong that I believed all we had to do was pray, and God would give us direction. Sam had absolutely no faith that prayer or anything else was going to change the situation. I challenged his unbelief with story after story in the Bible of all the miraculous things God had done, but Sam did not want to hear it. I was so frustrated with him because, to me, it seemed so simple. This was to become a recurring scenario that would play itself out over and over in the years to come.

Much to my dismay, Sam settled the dispute by signing a no-fault consent decree agreeing to represent less savings until he had third-party scientific proof. A year later, he had gotten the scientific proof from one of the largest engineering companies in the state of Texas. This legally allowed the company to go back to the original energy savings claims, but by then the damage had been done. Agreeing to the consent decree had given the impression that the company had been wrong in the first place. It was a PR disaster that would take us years to recover from.

In an attempt to salvage Eagle Shield, Sam bought out a new electronic pest control device called Electrocat. When plugged into an electrical wall socket, it would send a current through the wiring of the house that distressed the bugs. Once again the Attorney General's office came calling. They wanted independent, scientific proof that the device actually worked. Sam was bewildered because other similar products had been on the market for some time. Why were we being targeted? Lacking the energy or the resources to fight it, Sam was out of the pest control business as fast as he had gotten in it.

Though it was beginning to feel as if everything was piling up against us, Sam was convinced he could turn things around. I told him that what was happening was not about energy savings claims or pest control devices, but about following God. I believed that somehow God was using all of these circumstances to test our faith and obedience. Again, to me the answer was simple—if you want the company to turn around, then turn to prayer.

I read Sam the Scripture in Proverbs 3:5-6, which says, *"Trust in the Lord with all your heart and do not lean on your own understanding. In all your ways acknowledge Him, and He will make your paths straight."* I sincerely assumed if we trusted in these words, then God would show us what to do. Sam, however, was not yet ready to relinquish his understanding. He said his instincts had always worked in the past and that he would succeed again. Never having experienced failure in business before, Sam was convinced that this time around would be no different. Looking back, I can see that although God loved Sam's selfless heart, He was going to have to break his pride. This would not be easy for either of us.

Tough Times Getting Tougher

God was now beginning to give me insight or discernment into Sam's business dealings. I don't know how to explain it, but I would get feelings and have understanding about situations I had no foreknowledge of. As great as this may sound, it would take Sam and me several more years to understand how our separate spiritual and natural gifts could ever work together. It would take much pain, disenchantment, and anger to get us to where God needed us to be to fulfill the amazing destiny He had for our lives.

Our happy home was now in turmoil. I was constantly pushing Sam to rely on God, and I was totally frustrated that he wouldn't. Sam could not accept the fact that he was unable to make Eagle Shield's business problems work out, and he was tired of hearing me tell him how easy the solution could be.

Then came the final blow. In August 1989, radiant barrier hit the retail market nationwide in every major home improvement store. The price was thirty percent less than Eagle Shield's for the same product. Because Sam had no patents on the product to protect against such price competition, our sales plummeted by ninety percent in ninety days! We were forced to shut down the company.

Chapter Three

The Good,
The Bad,
The Blessing

In December 1989, we closed the doors on Eagle Shield, which was difficult, to say the least. Sam felt personally responsible for everyone. The business dropped so fast that it was not able to make its final payroll or commissions. Sam and I had about four hundred, twenty-five thousand dollars in the bank. After praying for direction we both felt that God wanted us to give the bulk of the money to the company. It would be a loan that we knew would never be repaid, but this amount would help cover the payroll, commissions, and many of the outstanding debts.

We believed this was good stewardship of "God's" money, so wrote a check for four hundred thousand dollars, leaving the remainder to start our business lives over again. Sam and I actually had a peace about the entire situation. The closing of the business relieved the pressure that had built between us, and giving that money was the first thing we had prayed about and agreed upon together in quite some time.

About two months after we gave our money to the company, Sam got a letter from the Internal Revenue Service. It stated that a mistake had been made in a previous return and that we now owed them one hundred thousand dollars! Sam was in shock. He questioned whether putting our money back into the company had been the right thing. Had we really heard from the Lord? I told Sam that this was an attack from the enemy to discourage us. I knew God had directed us to give the four hundred thousand dollars, so I had absolutely no doubt that He would deliver us from this problem. It was time to pray!

I read a Scripture in Isaiah 55:11 that says, *"So will My word be which goes forth from My mouth; it will not return to Me empty, without accomplishing what I desire, and without succeeding in the matter for which I sent it."* So, I boldly and with every ounce of faith I could possibly muster, took the Word of God to proclaimed victory over this situation with the IRS. Sam was now in greater shock than before. In total disbelief he said, "You can pray all you want, but we're dealing with the IRS!" He still did not understand the power of prayer and thought that I had gone over the edge. But finally, Sam realized there were no other options and reluctantly began to pray with me about it. We prayed together over this issue for the next two weeks, and in my heart, I believed that God had resolved our problem.

One day, shortly after that two-week prayer time, Sam walked in with another letter in his hands. This one was from a state agency, which claimed that upon review, Sam had paid too much state tax and was entitled to a refund. You cannot imagine what the amount was—one hundred thousand dollars and thirty-five cents! God had given us all the money we needed to pay the IRS and enough money for a stamp!

Still unconvinced about all this prayer stuff, Sam made a call to the accountants who had originally filed the state return. After investigating the situation, they told Sam that the state had made a mistake and to send the money back with a letter of explanation. With disappointment in his voice, Sam made a pessimistic comment about our miracle and returned the refund check. But I refused to relent and continued to pray harder.

It might sound hard to believe, but I was not the least bit discouraged. My trust and faith was completely in the Lord. Two weeks later the check came back from the state, this time with interest. Sam, at the advice of his accountants, sent it back a second time. My resolve grew stronger. What a spiritual fight must have been going on! A few more weeks passed, and once again the check came back to us. This time the accountants threw their hands up and said they had no explanation. They had never seen this sort of thing before. We finally cashed the check, paid the IRS, and thanked God for answering our prayer.

I'm convinced that God honored us in our faithfulness. The Bible states that if you are faithful with a little, God will entrust you with a lot.[1] I think God used that episode to test our faithfulness with "a little." What we did not realize then was just how much He would entrust to us in the future. But first He had to make sure we understood the difference between "faithful" and "foolish."

Putting that large amount of our own money back into the company to cover the last payroll and pay the final bills was not a problem for Sam because he has been blessed with a very giving heart. Although Sam has had lots of successes in his life, he has never been motivated by money. He loves to give everything he has to others. This may be one of his biggest assets, but it can also be one of his biggest liabilities. Sam's generosity has often been misguided. He would fall for one sad story after another and end up giving people money. I believed that sometimes Sam kept them from having to accept consequences for their choices. He was always there to bail them out, and I felt that many times Sam got in the way of God from working in their lives.

---

[1] Luke 16:10

Good Seed—Bad Ground

We were still relatively new Christians, but God had put us on a fast learning track. Sam met a man who was an usher at the new church we were attending. One day this man asked Sam to meet him for lunch and told him that he had been in legal trouble a few years back and was ordered by the court to pay financial restitution for his crime. This man had recently had a run of bad luck and had not made any payments for several months. Now he was in jeopardy of going to jail if he did not pay the full amount by the following Friday. This man's predicament pulled at Sam's heartstrings in a big way. How could he let a Christian brother go to jail? Without even telling me, Sam went to court with this man, wrote a check to the court in the amount of eight thousand dollars, and bailed the guy out. That was about half the money we had to our name.

When Sam told me what he had done, I was very upset, to say the least. He said that the man was going to sell his car the next week to repay him. I explained that we should have prayed and asked God whether it was His will for us to intervene in this man's life or not. I shared with Sam that God might have wanted this person to pay the consequences of his behavior instead of having us fix things for him. Because Sam made this decision from a deep place in his heart, he had a hard time believing he had done anything wrong. After all, he was helping out a person in need. The only thing I knew to do was to pray, and when I did, I knew immediately that this man would never pay us back.

As it turned out, not only did this man refuse to sell his car, he never even returned Sam's phone calls. I think God wanted Sam to learn that giving away your money without prayerful consideration is not good stewardship. Sam believed that because he could give so freely, it proved he was not owned by money and so God was pleased with him. But we have since discovered there is a fine line between giving by the leading of the Lord and giving because you cannot say no. I'm certain that God loved Sam's selfless heart and his true desire to bless others, but Sam's unhealthy reasons for giving would carry a high price in what God was preparing for our future.

Blessed Again!

Exactly one year and three days after Chad was born, our adorable daughter, Hannah Raye Caster, was born. Hannah was a beautiful baby with lots of dark, curly hair and big brown eyes. Sam and I were ecstatic that God had blessed us again. I cannot describe the joy

I felt as the mother of these precious children. Chad was too young to know what was going on, but, once again, Brooke was elated. Because we were so blessed personally, we were able to tolerate our business challenges. Our children helped us to keep things in perspective. All in all, our life was good once again.

Chapter Four

God's Plan Begins To Take Shape

A distant relative of Sam's had been working in a cancer program that was using an individualized nutritional approach as a key part of its treatment protocols. Sam had never met this lady, but through the family she had heard of Sam's marketing successes. She called Sam and asked if he would consult with her new company. They were trying to find the best way to take this unique program to market.

Sam visited their office and came home very excited. He did not know anything about nutrition but was amazed at how well their cancer patients had done. Over the next several months Sam dove into this project. He read everything they offered, even the training materials their technicians studied. Sam felt that he had found more than a business; he had found a cause.

God was now beginning to reveal things to me in very clear ways. I no longer just had a "sense" or a "feeling" about things; it was becoming much more than that. God would give me specifics about what would happen if Sam took one path or another. He began to reveal to me details about people, without my having ever met them. This knowledge seemed so natural that I was surprised other people didn't see it too. I have since come to understand that God was imparting to me a gift of revelation or knowledge.

In First Corinthians, chapter 12, the Bible explains clearly that God gives gifts to all of us, and these gifts are to be used for His glory, not our own. We are never to use them for self-exaltation or self-gain. All He is looking for is willing vessels.

Increased Gifting—Increased Frustration

As this gifting in me increased, it began to cause tension once again between Sam and me. One reason for this was because I did not know how to explain this discernment that I had. But another and even more frustrating reason was that Sam's gifts were also growing and they seemed to be in opposition to mine.

Sam had been praying for wisdom, and God was beginning to impart that gift to Sam in greater measure. He had a very strong sense that nutritional science was where God was leading him. Although I believed him, I knew that Sam was not supposed to be in business with this present company. This knowledge was so strong to me that I couldn't understand why Sam would not just pack up and leave immediately. Hadn't God's revelations through me been right in the past? I felt like Sam was not just ignoring me, but that he was also ignoring God's will. Sam would not yield and stayed with this company for almost another full year. Our mutual frustration only grew.

You can imagine the toll that year took on our personal lives. I responded by praying that God would stop revealing anything to me concerning Sam's businesses. I was very weary, and I did not want to hear any more. Life with our children was good, but in terms of business, Sam and I were on different planets. It would take us several more years of exasperating situations before we would finally learn how to blend our gifts together instead of opposing each other. It's amazing to reflect on those times of such grief and heartache and see how much God was truly maturing us in our own ways. We could not see it at the time, but everything was going according to God's design.

I must admit that in spite of those frustrating days, there was a bright point. It was at this nutritional company where Sam met Bill Fioretti. Bill was a biochemist, and he and Sam worked together on several projects. They developed a trust and respect for one another. Bill lived in San Antonio with his family, but during the week he stayed with us, returning home on weekends. He commuted like this for several months. We enjoyed having him as a guest because he was a kind, respectful, fun-loving person. In retrospect, had Sam left this nutritional company when I felt he should, he would not have met Bill. My insight had been right, but I had not yet learned to rely on God's timing. Like Sam, I would mature in my gifting also.

Bill would play a huge roll in Sam's future. Their laid-back, carefree approach to life provided Sam with some of the happiest times he ever had in a business relationship. But those same eager-to-please traits would one day cost them in ways they would never have believed.

Bill and Sam's Great Adventure

In early 1992, Sam and Bill left the nutrition company and started a new company to develop biotech products for animals. This was mainly Bill's project. He created a working relationship with the poultry science faculty at Louisiana State University, and their company began investing in the discovery of new technologies that could be patented.

While Bill was working with LSU, Sam was invited to meet with a non-profit organization called Kids 4 Tomorrow. They used former professional athletes to mentor at-risk children in the public school systems. Kids 4 Tomorrow was interested in Sam's ideas for fund raising. He visited their offices in Phoenix and was challenged to create an out-of-the-box concept for raising money. Sam told Bill about his meeting and suggested they start another company that would leverage their past experiences into a fund-raising platform for these athletes.

To be consistent with the athletes' mission of helping students, Sam decided they needed two types of products. The first one was a healthy, nutritious food bar that would benefit the students and their families, and could also be used for local school fund-raisers. The second item Sam chose was a newly developed home learning product pioneered by a Dallas based company called Lessonware. Their product, "The Study Game," used high-profile athletes like Joe Montana, Wayne Gretzky, and Chris Evert to teach children how to improve their study skills through a home video and workbook program.

Sam felt these two products were a great complement to the Kids 4 Tomorrow program and chose network marketing as the form of distribution for the products. A large percentage of their profits were allocated to Kids 4 Tomorrow. It was a totally unconventional way to raise money for a non-profit entity, but it worked. The company took off, and sales climbed briskly.

Bill's job was to organize and run the operations of the company. He also made frequent visits to LSU for their biotech company. I was sure God's hand was on this new venture, but it had been a while since I spent any time in prayer for Sam's business dealings. Once Sam made the decision to leave the nutrition company, our lives had mellowed out again. There were no external stresses and no conflicting agendas. I was glad that God was not giving me any insight into this new company. I was more than happy to stay out of Sam's way and let him make all the business decisions on his own. The company was exploding. Sam was back in his element, children were being helped, and all was well on the home front.

God's New Gift—Nausea

In the spring of 1993, Sam and I were on vacation in New England with Don and Lydia. While driving up the beautiful coast of Maine, Sam casually relayed a conversation he had the previous week with the CEO of Lessonware. Sam's company was responsible for about ninety percent of the sales of their product, The Study Game. Lessonware was a public company, trading on the penny stock market. Their board and CEO had decided that such significant sales to one vendor created a huge liability for their company. Their first choice to resolve the problem was to propose either a merger or a buy out of Sam and Bill's company.

Sam was really excited about the proposal. The merger buyout would convert Sam's company into a public company and increase the profit of selling the games. Sam was very upbeat when telling us about the proposal because he could see all those wonderful benefits. However, the minute Sam said the CEO's name with the word "merger," I felt sick to my stomach!

I did not know the CEO, and I didn't know much about his company, but I knew without a doubt that God was against such a move. This feeling was stronger than any feeling I had ever had before. I told Sam, "There is no way this merger is supposed to happen because I know it isn't God's will." To say Sam was stunned would be an understatement. He had already decided that this was going to be a great thing. He was probably already developing a whole new marketing plan in his head, and my statements put a screeching halt to that.

Sam's first comments were "How can you possibly feel so strongly about this? You've never even met the CEO? How can God give you such a strong sense like this? Don't you think you should at least meet the man before you just declare that the deal is dead?" I told Sam that I couldn't explain my reaction, and although I had not met this man, I had heard from God before and I knew I was hearing from Him now. Sam's day was ruined. Don and Lydia didn't quite know what to make of the whole ordeal, so our trip continued with very little discussion of the issue.

When we returned to Dallas, Sam asked me to think again about the merger. "Just come and meet this man, and then decide," he said. I said that God had made His decision perfectly clear to me and that I didn't need to meet anyone. I was frustrated that Sam did not trust my discernment. He was equally discouraged that I did not trust his business acumen.

I told Sam to do what he wanted because I had nothing else to offer. I was emotionally and spiritually drained. Our relationship was strained once again. I knew God's hand was on us, but I could not understand why He allowed this struggle to continue. Bill Fioretti was not in favor of the merger either, but he left the decision up to Sam. He was spending more and more time at LSU anyway.

Sam completed the buy out despite my protest. The new company's name became Lessonware Direct. Within weeks the Lessonware board decided to stop selling the nutritional bars. Sam could not believe it! It was the only consumable product they had, which meant it was the only product the distributors could reorder for personal consumption. The decision was based on the board's belief that nutrition played no role in a child's ability to study and besides, it "cheapened" their image. The board was also debating on whether to continue with the donations to Kids 4 Tomorrow. Sam was appalled at the arrogance and ignorance of these decisions, but unfortunately, he was getting little sympathy out of me.

The business was in trouble; yet the new owners refused to acknowledge the problem. They believed the business just needed to be purged from those "nutrition nuts" and handed over to those who recognized the value of higher learning. Within four months the new company was broke. Sam and Bill never received a payment on the sale of the business and salvaged only the office furniture, computers, and supplies.

Once again, Sam had "leaned on his own understanding" and would pay an ongoing price for his decision. It was not a financial burden that Sam would have to bear this time, but a stigma on his reputation. Now he had been involved in two failed companies. Competitors and detractors would leverage that against him from that point forward.

I didn't need to say, "I told you so." Sam understood what happened. He was beginning to see that the Midas touch of the past no longer seemed to work. Somehow, in spite of it all, I knew God was going to stand with Sam and use him to accomplish great things. This was not the end of Sam's career as a business leader. Not by a long shot.

Chapter Five

Birthed In Prayer

It was now the summer of 1993, and I was spending a lot of time in prayer. I didn't understand why, but from the time we became Christians, our businesses seemed to fail. One day the Lord spoke clearly to my heart about it. He said that although Sam and I had entrusted our marriage, our children, and our finances to Him, we had never entrusted our businesses to Him. Of course! That made perfect sense to me! I knew that to receive God's fullness, we had to trust Him completely, but somehow I never thought of it in terms of business.

I shared this new revelation with Sam. By now, because of all we had been through with our other ventures, Sam was more open when I spoke about spiritual issues. I told him that we earnestly needed to seek God's direction for our next business endeavor and that God needed to be a constant part of it.

Don Herndon had been involved with some of Sam's other businesses, and he was fully aware of our struggles. We decided to talk to him and Lydia about the insight that I had gotten from the Lord. That day, my mother, Ofilia plus the four of us, literally got on our knees and prayed. We had no idea what God had in store for us, but we declared that whatever it was, we would steward it in a way that was honoring to Him. We made a commitment to seek God's wisdom and direction and to serve Him in humility.

Knowing that my desire was to be a full-time mom and not to work in the business, I promised the Lord that my job would be to pray for the company. I also promised to be a mouthpiece for Him to declare His glory whenever He asked. I don't typically get pictures in my mind when I pray, but that day I did. I saw Sam and me on a large concert-type stage in a huge football-type stadium. It was filled with tens of thousands of people, and they were joyful and excited. I sensed that was a picture of the blessing that God was going to bestow on our next company, whatever it was to be.

The Lord, again, spoke to my heart and said that this next company was to be a "Joseph Company." Although I was somewhat familiar with the story of Joseph in the book of Genesis, I wasn't sure what God meant. It seemed a bit strange that God would lay that phrase (Joseph company) on my heart, but I later learned what a blessing it would be and how it would someday impact the lives of people of all races, of all faiths, and on all continents of the world.

As I look back over the last few years, I can now see the many similarities between the calling on Sam's and my life and the life of Joseph. God called Joseph to a purpose greater than he could have accomplished by himself. So were we. His journey to fulfill that purpose was littered with relational detours and political potholes. So was ours. God used Joseph to provide food to a world ravaged by famine. Through our new company, God used us to provide a new "manna" to a world ravaged by disease.

I felt God was going to place Sam at the head of this new company. Sam had been blessed with a sincere humility, a desire to serve, and a love for people. He had been blessed with an uncanny ability to find the right products and connect them to the perfect business model. He was not driven by greed or power. And, last but not least, he had become acquainted with the realities of spiritual warfare.

Once we dedicated our business to God, He was ready to fulfill His destiny for our lives. There was only one major obstacle we had to get around. Ourselves! Not only had Sam seen God work, he had also suffered the consequence of disobedience, and I was convinced he was ready to lean on God's understanding instead of his own. I should not have jumped to that conclusion so quickly... we still had a long way to go.

By October 1993, our prayers were answered. Sam and Bill decided the timing was right to go into the nutrition industry. The demand from consumers was growing, the laws were changing, and the use of good science provided an incredible opportunity to succeed like never before.

Bill had a great idea for their first product, which would later be named "PLUS." Bill contacted a friend of his to formulate and help manufacture the first run of product. This friend had a pharmaceutical business that had been in his family for about a hundred years. Sam and Bill thought this friend would provide a good strategic connection for future product development but also talked to him about becoming a partner in this new business. Sam loved the idea because it gave his new company instant credibility to be co-owned by such an established company. He and Bill were working out the ownership agreement while the first product was being manufactured.

My Nausea Returns

Sam came home and shared this exciting new strategy with me, and I immediately got that sick feeling in my stomach, much like I did when he told me about Lessonware. I recognized this as God's way of telling me that this plan was absolutely not supposed to happen. I told Sam of my feelings, and he just stood there and stared at me, speechless. Here he had helped mastermind this brilliant idea that would give the company instant credibility, and I was bursting his bubble – again! Little did I know that he had already begun negotiating the agreement. I reminded Sam that we prayed for God to provide everything to insure the success of the company, therefore, we did not need to bring in other partners in order to make our company credible.

By now, Sam had enough experience with these strange revelations of mine that he could not just brush them off, but I could tell that it was going against all of his instincts. Much to his credit, he reluctantly agreed that I might indeed have been given a word from God. I could see that the Lord was working in Sam's heart because the next day he went into the office and told Bill they needed to stop the negotiations with his friend. Although Bill didn't understand, he trusted Sam enough to agree with him. They then decided to use the man only as a manufacturer of their product.

A few weeks later the first product arrived. Bill took some of the bottles from that first shipment and had them tested by an independent lab. Bill had formulated the product with an herb called Dioscorea. Only a few species of this herb contain the active ingredient that provides its health benefit, and Bill had specifically designated that the new product be standardized with a minimum amount of that component. It would cost a premium for the raw material, but Bill knew that the quality was much more critical than the price.

When the test results came back, the amount of active ingredient was way below what Bill and his friend had agreed to. When Bill confronted him, the friend immediately attacked Bill's lab results and challenged their friendship. The bottom line was that this man was trying to cheat the company with a cheap, ineffective product, but he failed to realize that Bill would have it tested. The relationship ended only a few weeks after this "friend" was to become a stockholder and partner in the company. The incident drew Sam and me closer together. We had passed a major test, and this time we could celebrate together.

Detouring The Destiny

Now Bill and Sam were ready to finalize the ownership structure of the new company. Bill, feeling the new company could use an infusion of capital, encouraged Sam to consider letting his cousin, Skip, invest some money in return for some ownership. Sam was eager to please and, in essence, agreed to a three-way split of the ownership. Sam just could not understand the leadership role that God had called him to, and this move would not only cost him control of the company, but would derail God's intended direction for it.

This may sound like a broken record, but I was once more distraught over yet another "Sam" decision. I had a sick feeling that we had moved away from God's perfect will. Sam had not consulted me about Skip's role in the company. He had not prayed about it; he just did it. This time Sam's lack of discernment had caused him to give away control of what God had entrusted to him alone. We didn't know it then, but it would be seven very hard years before God would restore him to his rightful place.

Sam and I prayed about a name for the new company and, with the help of Bill and a few others, we came up with the name "Emprise," which means a bold and chivalrous journey. The business began with some great people. Ray Robbins, who had been in two of Sam's previous companies, helped Sam with the development of a marketing plan and took on the role of National Sales Director. Sam took on the position of President, and Bill was the CEO.

Ray helped recruit another incredible business builder named Jett. These two men were relentless in their efforts to get the sales and recruiting off the ground. My mother Ofilia Mullens, Don Herndon, Steve Hames, Jason Mallett, Dick Hankins, Kim Snyder, and Missy Thompson made up the opening office staff, and things began to build. Without this great group of people, I don't know how we would have ever made it. They were all willing to work for very little pay, but it was worth it to them because they saw the potential in this new company.

Bill was inspired with many ideas for products. One of the unique items that Bill formulated was a children's product, Phyto-Bears, which is a combination of flash-dried fruit and vegetable extracts in a gummi-bear form. Today, that idea has become one of our best selling products and has been featured on such television programs as Good Morning America. It also was named one of the Top Ten best new products of 1996, out of a field of 26,000!

God's Way—Not Man's

One of our associates, Lowell Thomas, had managed to introduce our new products to a group of world-class track and field athletes at the University of Houston. They were all experiencing great success with our products. Sam went with Lowell to visit them and asked them for an endorsement in exchange for free product. We had decided that we would not pay any endorsement fees because we believed that God would bring the right people at the right time to the company.

All of these track and field athletes were Olympic medal winners, including Leroy Burell, who at that time held the world record in the 100 meters. Sam explained what the company was willing to do, and all the athletes agreed. Sam was excited and started making plans to promote their endorsements, but later in the week, he received a call from Leroy Burell's agent. He told Sam that since his client currently held the distinction of being the fastest man on earth, Emprise would have to pay ten thousand dollars for the endorsement as well as a royalty on product sales.

Sam called me from work about some other matter, and he mentioned the call from Burell's agent. He said there was probably some negotiating room, so he was working on a counter offer. I then reminded Sam of our previous commitment not to pay for endorsements and of our prayer to trust in God to bring the people we needed. He said that although he remembered our agreement, this was different "After all," Sam said, "We're talking about the world-record holder in the 100 meters." I said, "Well, if we've decided not to trust God anymore, go ahead and make your deal." Even though he could have justified this as a legitimate exception, Sam said he wanted to trust the Lord, and with that, he turned down the agent's offer.

Sam was really struggling with relying on God instead of his own instincts, but at least he was beginning to recognize it and fight off the temptation. Sam believed God would provide someone else, but he thought it was a shame to lose such a high-profile endorsement. It never occurred to Sam that God might have a better plan.

Later in the week, Leroy Burell called back and said that he felt drawn to the company and its mission in a way that he could not explain, and he wanted to be a part of it. He offered his endorsement for no fee. Sam was now beginning to understand how this deal with God was going to work. He was going to have to move over and let God lead him. The Leroy Burell incident had been a huge faith builder for both of us.

From The Fastest Man To The Biggest Heart

In the spring of 1994, God answered our prayer in a huge way by sending us a local doctor by the name of Reg McDaniel. Reg was not your typical M.D. in any sense of the word.

Dr. Reg had served on the boards of area hospitals, had been Chief of Staff and Chief of Pathology at a hospital in Grand Prairie, Texas, sat on the Texas State Board of Education, and had been named "Physician of the Year" by his colleagues. But most providentially for our company, Reg had been the consulting doctor in a series of pilot studies using a patented aloe vera extract on AIDS patients. The results of those studies completely changed Reg's thinking about natural remedies, and he had spent the last several years telling anyone who would listen about the product.

Reg's heart was as big as Texas—so big in fact, that he even ran a free clinic for patients whose insurance had run out, giving them this aloe product to support their ongoing recoveries. For this work, instead of being honored by his peers, they ridiculed Reg for supporting this alternative approach. But Reg knew he was truly called to a higher purpose, so he cared little about what others thought. To his patients, he had become a saint. He was a doctor, not ruled by insurance companies and hospital profit structures. Reg was motivated by a passion to help others.

After being introduced to Emprise by Ray Robbins, Dr. Reg met with Sam for an entire afternoon, and before they were through, he had encouraged Sam to license the rights to Manapol, the patented aloe vera product he had helped research. Sam instantly convinced Bill that this was the way to lock up a patented product with broadbase customer appeal. An agreement was put together almost immediately with the manufacturer of Manapol.

Right after the deal was signed, giving Emprise exclusive rights to Manapol, Reg surprised us all by asking Sam if he could join the Emprise team to help tell the story of this amazing product. Sam explained that the company did not have enough money to pay a doctor of Reg's caliber. Reg responded by saying, "Pay me what you can, when you can. This story is too important to worry about the money."

Few of us ever have the privilege of meeting someone who has such a deep love for people. Reg McDaniel is one of those unique finds, and he became Sam's hero almost overnight. Sam and Reg were like kids in a candy store. Every week in those early days they would meet to review the latest miracles they had heard from product users and associates during their meetings around the country or on national conference calls. Their mutual respect for each other's talents and skills bonded them together in a way that is hard to explain.

In God's master plan for this Joseph Company, Reg McDaniel was to play a key role with his ability to touch so many lives through his message of hope. God was also going to use Reg to evolve this aloe extract into a new complex that would become one of God's true gifts of provision for health to the world.

Chapter Six

A Name Change— God's Fingerprint

By now, Skip Fioretti had entered the scene. Skip sold his interest in some restaurants and came to Texas to join Emprise. Bill was struggling to balance his CEO duties with Emprise and his work with LSU. Skip had prior experience in running a restaurant chain so he relieved Bill by taking over the CEO position. This made him a salaried executive as well as a major stockholder.

Shortly after Skip's arrival, an attorney representing Emprise Bank in Kansas contacted the company. They claimed that they owned the rights to the name "Emprise" and that we were causing confusion in the market place. Our attorneys said that two companies with the same name could coexist, like Delta Faucets and Delta Airlines for example, as long as their businesses were different, which obviously ours were. Skip, Sam, and our trademark attorneys flew to Kansas to meet with the CEO and their legal counsel, in an attempt to reach a logical agreement allowing both parties to utilize the name. However, the bankers said they would not back down on their demand and that we needed to change our name or meet them in court. While there seemed to be no room for compromise, everyone agreed to meet the next morning for further discussion.

Sam and I talked by phone that night and prayed for God's favor in this situation. Early the next morning Sam called back and said he felt God had given him a strategy when he woke up. This was really strange to Sam because he felt like God had never given him such clear direction before. What God told Sam to do was also way out of his comfort zone, but, out of obedience, he was willing to do it. Sam said he believed God wanted him to tell the bankers the story of how our company was prayed into existence and the calling that had been placed on it. He said he was also supposed to tell them that through prayer, we had been given the name "Emprise" for our company.

Sam asked what I thought of the idea, and I told him that I thought he had indeed gotten direction from God. I was positive that God had given him the very message he was to deliver. Because Sam had seen the Lord do so many tremendous things in the past, he felt this would be a great witness to everyone present. When everyone met that morning, even though he was nervous about what he was going to say, Sam asked if he could make the opening address. He said he just wanted to put some perspective on what was being asked by the bank. They agreed to let Sam open the discussion.

Sam shared from his heart all that God had instructed him to say. After he finished giving his message, both sides sat there for several moments just staring at him. Finally, the CEO for the bank said, "Although that was an interesting story, it has no relevance to these discussions." Both parties stated the merits of their legal positions, and the debate was on.

Sam called me on their lunch break, totally devastated. He said he had never been so embarrassed. Surely it hadn't been God that had asked him to do such a foolish thing, or the result would have been different. I asked him to try to recall exactly what he had heard God speak to his heart. He repeated basically everything he had said earlier with the addition of one more thing. Sam concluded that if he delivered the message, God would change the minds of the bankers and let him keep the name "Emprise."

It suddenly became apparent to Sam that this had been an assumption on his part. God had told him to deliver the message—period. There had been no promise of keeping our name. Sam had obeyed the Lord and, based on that, I tried to encourage him by saying that God must have another plan for us. I said that everything would work out exactly as it was supposed to and that God would give us a better name.

The bank did not yield. Our attorneys suggested it would be better to change our name rather than take on an expensive court battle. Sam had gone way out on a limb to honor what he believed God had asked him to do. I knew God was pleased with him. The setback to this was that the one time Sam felt like he had gotten direction from God, it seemed to backfire. He was very cautious from then on about saying or believing that God "spoke" to him.

God will reveal His plans to us in many different ways. All He asks of us is to be obedient and to trust Him completely. We don't always know what the outcome will be, but we are to obey nevertheless. God loves it when we spend time communicating with Him through prayer, praise, or reading His Word. The more we do these things, the more we know Him, and the stronger our faith becomes. I was so proud of Sam for acting in faith on what the Lord had told him to do.

Manna – A Prophetic Name

When Sam returned home, we prayed for a name. That night Sam woke up, and God led him to read Numbers, chapter 11, which talks about manna. It was then that Sam came up with the name "Mannatech." Sam presented the new name to management, and they agreed to it. No other names were even brought up. It was announced to the associates, and that was the end that.

The name change was an amazingly smooth transition. Most people said they liked it better than the old name. I had read several stories in the Bible of God changing people's names, such as Abram to Abraham[2] or Jacob to Israel[3]. I realized that when He did that, it was because they were about to go through some significant changes in their lives and also to receive a great blessing. I believed that was the reason God changed our name.

Shortly after the name change, Sam received a call from an associate named Donna Kuntz, who told him that she had been to a conference, several months before, where she heard a man speak on the subject of prophetic gifting. The speaker said that one prophetic word he had been given was that God would raise up a nutritional company, but it was going to be used for spiritual warfare* against the plans of the enemy. He said the company would have the word "Manna" in its name. Donna told Sam that when he announced that Mannatech was the new name of the company, chills ran down her spine as she recalled that prophetic word. Needless to say, we shared Donna's reaction completely and were thrilled with its confirmation to Sam's "choice!"

If we ask, God will always confirm His will to us. He wants us to know we're doing the right thing. There's a story in the book of Judges, in chapter 6, about a man named Gideon who asked God for confirmation before he obeyed, and God gladly gave it to him. God told Gideon that He was going to use him and a small army to save Israel from its enemies. Gideon (in Judges 6:37) put a fleece of wool on the ground and said, *"If there is dew on the fleece only, and it is dry on all the ground, then I will know that You will deliver Israel through me, as You have spoken."* The next morning, sure enough, the fleece was wet, and the ground was dry. Gideon asked God one more time for confirmation. He asked God this time to make the fleece dry but make the ground wet. God, again, gave Gideon his answer with a dry fleece and wet ground.

God has been faithful to Sam and me by giving us confirmations like Donna's prophecy many times. Such confirmations have been a constant source of comfort to us when we've had to make difficult decisions.

---

[2]Genesis 17:5
[3]Genesis 32:28

*(Let me explain what I mean by "spiritual warfare." Just as God has a plan for our lives, Satan does also. In 1 Peter 5:8, we are warned that, *"Your adversary, the devil prowls around like a roaring lion, seeking someone to devour."* The Bible is clear about evil forces existing in the spiritual realm and that they have substantial influence on the world and human events. Their objective is to subvert the purposes of God. I have come to understand that God's plan in Mannatech is to bless people abundantly in their health, finances, and overall quality of life. Our "enemy" wants the complete opposite for our lives. He will use any means possible such as discouragement, frustration, and fear to keep us from receiving the fullness of God.)

Chapter Seven

A Company
Of Provision

In the autumn of 1994, Don and Lydia along with Sam and I, were invited to a Bible study by some people from the corporate office. David Colister and Bill Greenman were new employees who had previously been pastors. They led the study that first night, and soon it turned into a weekly meeting. I grew so much during this time and I enjoyed learning about the Bible from a perspective that was new to me. I learned to take my limitations off of God, and the importance of taking my prayer life to a deeper intensity. As a group, we spent a lot of time in prayer and as a result, we saw many answers to those prayers—especially for Mannatech.

It was with this group that I came to understand what God meant when He said that Mannatech would be a Joseph Company. The story of Joseph begins in the 37th chapter of Genesis. It's a fascinating story of trials, tribulations, heartache, and eventual victory. Joseph had correctly prophesied that there would be a worldwide famine. God had given him the foresight to store grain for seven years before the famine began, and, as a result, Joseph was able to provide food to all the surrounding nations for the next seven years. He provided to all the people who came to him, regardless of their spiritual beliefs, culture, or race.

This was also when I began to encounter the warfare God had spoken of in the prophecy Donna Kuntz had shared with us. As a new Christian, on fire for the Lord, I had promised God that I would be a mouthpiece for Him. My faith in God was not something intangible, it was the foundation of who I was and I looked forward to sharing my exuberance from the stage at our company events. Much to my surprise my speaking was met with great resistance from a handful of our field associates. Several times after Mannatech-sponsored events those who objected confronted me about using the stage to "promote my personal religious views." They said they joined the company for the business opportunity, not to hear about Jesus, and they further explained that the offensive nature of my speech would keep them from inviting others to our meetings. On the other hand literally hundreds of associates told me that it was my strong witness for Jesus that confirmed to them that they were in the right place.

Sam took an enormous amount of heat from some field leaders, as well as from corporate management, on this issue. He always responded with a tremendous amount of grace and sensitivity to those in opposition. Sam felt Mannatech should always promote an open environment, which allowed all people the freedom to express their reasons for being in the company, no matter what their faith or purpose. Sam defended my right, as a co-founder, to freely express my purpose, calling and beliefs the same as anyone else.

Sam's Greatest Gift

Sam is definitely a peacemaker and has such a heart for people. He wants to do the right thing for everybody so he was stuck between a rock and a hard place on this issue. Management at Mannatech tried to pressure Sam into removing me from the stage in order to stop the controversy, but Sam would not give in. Had Sam not been such an integral part of the business, I believe the board would have fired him for resisting their demands.

The pressure from this issue continued to build until Sam began to proclaim from stage that while it was our personal faith in God that called us to start this company, it was also our belief that it would take people of all faiths to accomplish God's purpose for the company. To some, he seemed to be compromising his faith, but now I can look back and see that God had definitely given Sam real insight into the "Joseph calling" on Mannatech.

The Bible tells us that Joseph was used by God to show his love for humanity by saving them from starvation during a worldwide famine. Joseph gave provision to all the people who needed it, regardless of their faith or position. This seven-year famine would have destroyed most of the world without Joseph's interpretation of Pharaoh's dream and his subsequent obedience to that interpretation. Consequently, Pharaoh placed Joseph in a governmental-type position, a CEO of sorts and he operated in that position with the wisdom and authority of the Lord. Likewise, God equipped Sam with the spiritual components of wisdom and authority in a business arena.

I can now see that years ago, through his successes and tribulations, through the mountain tops and the valleys, that God was preparing Sam to lead the charge in this modern-day Joseph story. Like most of the people God has chosen throughout the ages, Sam would appear to the "world" to be an unlikely candidate for that role. He never finished college, he has never had experience in the world's financial community, and he was raised without the benefits of status, wealth or connections. But for as long as I've known him, Sam's had an unbelievable "feel" for how to bring new technology to market. It's a God-given talent that he could never have learned in school or gotten from a book.

In spite of his admitted failure to follow God's direction, God has chosen to use Sam in a very significant way. One of the greatest commandments is "to love one another," and Sam does that more sincerely than anyone I have ever known. Sam saw, long before anyone else, that God's purpose for Mannatech was to bless the lives of millions of hurting, and sometimes hopeless, people around the world through a gift that had been entrusted to us. God was about to pour out a gift of provision to people of all faiths, and Sam would be called to take this gift to the nations. His initial sense of that vision enabled him to get beyond people's religious views or ideology and see them through the eyes of the Lord.

People may not have agreed with our personal faith, but Sam was able to connect them to the passion of our purpose. I believe people feel God's love through Sam, and, as a result, it has allowed him the ability to lead without making others feel threatened or condemned. He has a genuine servant's heart. Sam may have been slow in understanding how God worked through me, but he was quick to grasp the Joseph anointing that God had placed on him.

Chapter Eight
The Foundational Gift

Exodus 16:14,15,31 says that when the dew was gone, thin flakes like frost on the ground appeared on the desert floor. When the Israelites saw it, they said to each other, *"What is it?"* for they'd not seen anything like it before. Moses said to them, *"It is the bread which the Lord has given you to eat."* The people of Israel called the bread "manna." It was white like coriander seed and tasted like wafers made with honey or oil, and it was what God used to sustain the Israelites for forty years. Through this miracle called "manna," God showed his unconditional love and blessing on His children.

Today we live in a world ravaged by disease. AIDS is predicted to wipe out millions of people on the continents of Africa and Asia. Cancers, heart disease, and hundreds of newly discovered disorders are ruining the lives of millions on every other continent. I believe that with Mannatech, God wants to pour out His blessing on mankind again through what I consider to be "modern-day manna." I have personally witnessed the testimonies of thousands of lives that have been changed, some dramatically, through this provision.

God's Plan Is Birthed

Another miracle from God is how I would describe what follows. There is an amazing similarity between the gift of provision God gave to the starving Israelites as they wondered in the desert, and what we were to be entrusted with to help a hurting world. The following story is really another story in itself and will again astonish you as you see how God's plan for this company started more than a decade before we prayed in my mother's living room for the company, which became Mannatech. I have had to depend on others for most of the facts which follow, as much of it occurred without Sam's or my involvement.

In the early 1980's, Dr. Bill McAnalley, a research pharmacologist, was hired by a group of investors to try to isolate the medically active ingredient in the aloe vera plant. History had established aloe vera as the world's most popular and well-known plant for healing. The problem was that commercially processed aloe did not produce the same level of health benefits that fresh aloe vera gel did. These investors wanted to know what caused the unique benefits and why they eroded when processed.

After much research, Dr. McAnalley discovered that the active ingredient in the aloe vera gel was a long-chain carbohydrate made up predominately of a sugar called Mannose. He also discovered that within a day or two after the aloe leaf is picked, this long-chain sugar molecule rapidly begins to disintegrate, causing the gel to lose much of its effectiveness. Dr. McAnalley then developed and patented a new way of processing the aloe vera gel that protected this long-chain sugar from being destroyed. This new stabilized aloe extract was then made available to the public in the form of a juice, and the testimonies began to flow.

People with all kinds of health problems began reporting their improvement after taking the new product, and the investors knew they had their hands on something significant. Because the law prohibited them from using testimonies in marketing the product as a "food," they decided instead to incorporate and bring this new technology to market as a drug. Years of research was done to validate the effectiveness of this new aloe extract for enhancing the function of the immune system. Pilot studies on AIDS patients were even initiated at a regional hospital under the direction of Reg McDaniel, M.D.

All the research data showed very positive results, and Dr. McAnalley was instructed to proceed with a drug application. But there was one big problem in this process. A new drug application requires the applicant to identify the complete chemical structure of the new drug. This required Dr. McAnalley to first extract the long-chain sugar molecule from the aloe extract and then show its chemical structure. These carbohydrate molecules consisted of thousands of individual sugars, linked together in a very complex structure.

Carbohydrate structuring was a brand new science in the mid 1980's and was only being taught at one or two universities in the world. Dr. McAnalley had no idea what to do next, and the project came to a halt. But Bill was not about to quit. He said that in his initial research on aloe vera, he had found several references to the plant in the Bible. Bill felt he had made his discovery with divine intervention. He felt that God's hand was on the project, and he prayed that somehow God would help him through his current dilemma. God heard him loud and clear.

The very next Saturday, Dr. McAnalley was working alone in his lab in the midst of a driving rainstorm. He heard a loud knock on the front door. When he opened it, a UPS driver was standing there with a drenched, but professionally dressed, man from Africa. The African explained that he had been dropped at the wrong address by a cab driver, and while standing in the rain had been picked up by the UPS driver. The driver went to his next stop to see if they could use a phone to call another cab. The next stop happened to be Dr. McAnalley's lab.

Dr. McAnalley invited the drenched man in to use his phone and struck up a conversation with him. The African said he had just received his Ph.D. and was on his way to a job interview with a large pharmaceutical company, when the taxi driver dropped him at the wrong location. Dr. McAnalley asked what kind of job he was interviewing for. The man explained that he had to settle for a job in quality control because he could not find work in his chosen field, which was a very new area of science. Dr. McAnalley then asked what that field was, and the man said that he had "recently graduated from a foreign university with a degree in carbohydrate structuring!" Isn't God amazing! Dr. McAnalley hired the scientist from Africa, and the project was on again.

The pharmaceutical company Dr. McAnalley was with found success in the late 80's and early 90's with a highly effective line of wound care products and received over one hundred worldwide patents on their aloe discovery. However, their attempt to create an approved drug from aloe proved very problematic. Technical obstacles, coupled with the millions of dollars in research required to validate a new drug, made the issue seem insurmountable.

To help generate income for their research, the company tried every way possible to sell their patented, food-grade aloe product, Manapol. They had the most effective aloe vera product on the market but could not generate sales. They placed their patented aloe products on the shelves of stores all over the country, and nothing happened. Their unique processing and stabilization of aloe vera was very costly therefore their finished product was more expensive than all the other aloe products. With little or no advertising budget, they had no way to inform consumers of their products.

The Plan Begins To Emerge

By 1994, Dr. McAnalley's employers were desperate for cash flow and were willing to license the exclusive rights to Manapol for the right price. In May of that same year, Ray Robbins brought Dr. Reg McDaniel to meet with Sam. Sam felt Mannatech had the perfect business model to market this product to consumers, and once again he was absolutely right. Bill Fioretti soon blended Manapol with Lecithin, and the new product was called Man-Aloe. Our associates embraced the product enthusiastically and within a matter of weeks they made it our number one seller. In fact, Mannatech sold more Manapol in its first month than the company who created it had sold in the prior six years. These sales were fueled by the hundreds of phenomenal testimonies we began to hear from people using the products and the energetic work of our associates.

The next divine appointment occurred when Dr. McAnalley finished his contract with the aloe pharmaceutical company and joined Mannatech. He, like Dr. McDaniel, saw that Mannatech could get their discoveries to market faster and more cost effectively than all the traditional approaches they had tried. God was bringing together all the people who would fulfill His destiny for Mannatech. It was an awesome thing to be a part of and to watch.

With the exclusive rights to Manapol, Mannatech's business tripled two years in a row. By 1996, sales reached almost one hundred million dollars. At Mannatech National Events the testimonies of people's miraculous recoveries from various health problems became overwhelming both in number and in substance. We would sit, literally for hours, and listen to one story after another of life-changing experiences. I was amazed to hear that so many people gave God all the glory for these miracles. We knew God had blessed Mannatech with one of the most miraculous products ever found to relieve human suffering. We would soon find out that an even greater blessing of "manna" was still to come.

Chapter Nine

Inspired New Manna

It is impossible to reflect on the following events and not marvel at the miraculous way in which God's plan unfolded. I say this so that as you read on, you will have a full appreciation of exactly how God was working. No man could orchestrate the following events.

In June of 1996, Dr. Reg and Dr. Bill went to Alexandria, Virginia, to make a presentation on their aloe product at The Second Annual International Congress of Alternative and Complementary Medicine, sponsored by Mary Ann Liebert Publishing Company. Reg had been sharing with Bill his belief that the sugar molecule in aloe vera might just be one of many other biologically "active" sugars needed by the body. While at this meeting in Virginia, during breakfast, Reg explained to Bill where his belief originated.

He told Bill that he had a strange dream. Reg said the dream was like a Power Point presentation. Each slide in the "dream" presentation revealed how various sugars were assembled and utilized in the cell. Bill was intrigued with Reg's revelation, and they both discussed the need to find the money to research the possible efficacy of other sugars.

While at breakfast, a young-looking man, with white hair, striking blue eyes, and dressed in an iridescent blue suit, was suddenly standing next to them. As they looked at him, he called them by name and said, "Dr. McDaniel, Dr. McAnalley, go to booth 129 (at the convention). They have what you need and are looking for." They looked at each other and then back at the man in blue—but he was gone!

In fact, he had disappeared from the restaurant in that split second of time! They were stunned and speechless. They had never seen this man before. No one, other than themselves, knew anything about their discussions on sugars. The man had disappeared before they could ask a single question, leaving them bewildered.

When the exhibition hall opened later that morning, Bill and Reg went directly to booth 129. Herbal remedies were displayed on one side of the booth, and piles of books and literature lay on the other. There were two young men manning the booth. Bill and Reg asked the two if any of their products on display contained sugars or aloe. None did. They looked through all the books and pamphlets in the booth, yet found nothing. Discouraged, but not ready to give up so quickly on the message they had received from the man with white hair, the doctors asked the two young men if there were possibly any other products or materials they might look over. One of the youth said they had a few boxes of odds and ends behind the booth and would see what he could find.

After several minutes he returned with a brown bottle containing a powdery substance called "Arabinogalactan." This is a freeze-dried powder from the sap of the larch tree that is rich in particular sugars. Bill asked if they had any literature on this substance. The man went out to check and came back with two research papers written by scientists in Germany, complete with the English translations. Reg and Bill stood there dumfounded. Just as the man in the blue suit had told them, what they found at booth 129 was the exact research which proved Reg's theory that there were other complex carbohydrates needed by the body.

Reg and Bill have no idea who the white-haired messenger was, how he knew their names, or how he knew what they needed. I believe that man was an angel. Both Dr. McDaniel and Dr. McAnalley have said many times in public that what had been placed in their hands was a gift from God. But just in case you might have any question about God's perfect timing, read on, because this story is far from over.

God Is Just In Time

While Bill and Reg were at this meeting, the aloe company that had licensed Manapol to Mannatech announced that they were going to introduce a new "food-grade" aloe product to the market. This would create competition for Manapol, which to Sam was, first and foremost, a huge ethics violation of their agreement, and, secondly, a probable violation of their exclusive contract. But Sam also felt that, from a PR perspective, having to sue their key supplier to stop this action might be even worse. Things looked hopeless.

Sam met with Reg and Bill, upon their return, and shared the devastating news. (Reg later told me that he had never seen Sam so dejected.) Sam was confused. How could God have orchestrated all that had happened and just allow it to be snatched away like this? What Sam did not realize was that on their way home from the convention, Bill and Reg were talking about different ways to use their new discovery. Should they pursue it now or should they wait? After hearing the bad news from Sam, they both agreed that they had been given the answer. They would provide the new formula to Mannatech.

By adding the additional biological sugars to Manapol, they had in their hands the next generation manna product. Bill McAnalley, with the help of chemist Eric Moore, formulated the new product and within sixty days, it was available for production. The name given to the new product was Ambrotose. About the same time, the

1996, 24th edition of Harper's Biochemistry was published. It validated everything that Reg and Bill had seen in Virginia by showing the body's need for eight specific complex sugar molecules. Bill and Reg had already included each of those sugars, or their precursors, in Ambrotose.

Because they were the first to recognize the nutritional benefit of this complex, they were able to file worldwide "composition of matter" patents on Ambrotose, giving Mannatech sole rights for its sale. God had delivered again with His miraculous timing.

Ambrotose was introduced before the aloe company could even begin the development of their new aloe product (which, by the way, they abandoned). Mannatech, in just sixty days, was set free from the unethical plan of its key vendor and gifted with its own proprietary technology. Dr. McAnalley had the new product tested at Texas Tech University, and it dramatically out performed Manapol and other aloe products. Then came the testimonies.

Individuals who had not responded well to the aloe alone began seeing a marked improvement in their health with Ambrotose. We all knew, without a doubt, that God had blessed us with something special—again. To me, Ambrotose is today's truest version of manna. I believe that it's a food complex straight from the hand of God to sustain and protect us. In the years since Ambrotose was discovered, tens of thousands of individuals have had their lives dramatically impacted by this extraordinary, natural complex.

The Third Wise Man

Not surprisingly, God delivered another "key" individual to our company. A Mannatech associate, Ferris Haddad, invited Dr. Steve Nugent, who was then President of the American Naturopathic Medical Association, to attend a national Mannatech event in Orlando, Florida. Sam invited Steve to make a short presentation on the value of Mannatech's products and how he came to believe in them. Before his message was over, Dr. Nugent had captured the hearts of our associates, and Sam knew that Steve was called to champion our cause with us. A short time later, Dr. Nugent joined Mannatech full-time. Since then he has blessed tens of thousands with his passionate gift of speaking on nutrition. Like Dr. McDaniel and Dr. McAnalley, Dr. Nugent provided yet another invaluable perspective for the future of Mannatech.

Dr. McAnalley often says that none of us can take any credit for the phenomenon Mannatech has become. I agree. In the next few years, we would be challenged with the stewardship of this important gift more than once. God was going to prosper all of us finan-cially, but He would call us to an even greater purpose than merely selling products. It would become our Joseph calling.

Chapter Ten

The Warfare Begins

When I refer to the enemy, I'm not talking about any individual. I'm talking about spiritual warfare. The Bible says that our enemy, Satan, comes into our lives to steal, kill, and destroy anything he can. I believe the devil will use anyone, through pride, selfishness, or arrogance, to accomplish his purpose. Even good men can be deceived. We are all vulnerable to those temptations, which can remove us, temporarily or permanently, from God's plan. I believe that Ambrotose is God's provision to bring healing on many different levels and that our enemy will stop at nothing to halt the blessing the Lord intends it to be.

I've struggled to understand this unpleasant truth, just as I'm sure many of you have. But again, the Bible is very clear on how and why this happens. There are many stories of how men and women, from all walks of life, fell into temptation because of fear, envy, pride, and love of money. God not only wants us to learn from their mistakes, but He also wants us to see His grace and mercy at work in their lives and to experience that for ourselves.

I'm writing this segment, not to be "preachy," but to help put into spiritual perspective, the events which follow. I'll mention several individuals who played a big role in what I believe was Satan's plan to bring this company to its end. I'm not accusing anyone of being evil or judging them in any way; in fact, I pray that God will touch their lives like He has ours. I'm simply trying to provide an explanation of how I believe spiritual warfare is carried out in our lives.

By the beginning of 1997, the upper management of the company was beginning to change dramatically as Skip Fioretti took control. The first thing he did was bring in new board members, and served as its chairman. Skip next promoted Pat (a friend of Bill Fioretti's) to CFO; hired a new CEO (Ron, a friend of Pat's); a new COO (Tony, a friend of Skip's from a previous business); a new company attorney named Deanne; a new VP of operations (Peter, Skip's brother-in-law); and Peter's friend, Patrick, as VP of Information Technologies (IT). All of these changes happened without objection from Sam. Since he didn't want the job of running administration, he felt that Skip had the right to bring in the people he wanted for those positions. However, Sam also trusted that Skip would leave the leadership and direction of the company to him. After all, he and Bill had successfully worked this way. They had complete respect and understanding for one another's skills and never got in each other's way.

Blinded To The Truth

Since I believed that God wanted Sam at the helm of the company, I was very uncomfortable with these personnel changes. I could feel the control of Mannatech slipping out of our hands, and I felt that Sam would soon be completely powerless. Sam didn't see things that way. He sincerely thought that sound business decisions were being made and that I was overreacting. I became increasingly frustrated with Sam's lack of concern for my uneasiness on this issue.

Fortunately, we had our prayer group to lean on. We got together with them on a weekly basis to talk and pray for direction. They gave us so much support and strength that I don't know how we would have made it without them. It seemed that each week God encouraged us about the company and re-energized our hope.

It did not take long for things at the office to change. The new regime began to assert more and more authority and push Sam further and further away. One thing that our entire prayer group felt was that Sam needed to go into the office and establish the spiritual authority that God had granted him. But Sam could not understand how he was supposed to do that. In reality, he was only a minority owner, and now Skip, along with Bill, controlled the company. Sam felt tremendous pressure from our group to take a stand and soon became reluctant to bring any Mannatech issues to us. He was frustrated with the way things were going at the company as well, but he had no idea how to fix any of it.

Sam invited Ron, the new CEO, to one of our group's prayer sessions. He only stayed for a short time and then had to leave. After meeting him that night, several of us felt that Ron would not be with the company for very long. We prayed for God's will in his life and for his time at Mannatech.

With the support of Skip, the new CEO began to push Sam out of the picture as much as possible. This culminated when they decided it was time to bring in a "professional" VP of sales to take over Sam's responsibilities. The management explained to Sam that he had taken the company as far as he was capable of, and now it was now time to put the company into more competent hands. Actually, Ron got the support of some associates who felt Sam had been too much of a deal-maker. Sam built the company in his entrepreneurial way of doing business, and Ron convinced people that was no way to run a business. The new management objected to Sam's commitment to pay Ray Robbins travel expenses. They also presumed that Sam was overly influenced by associate leaders. While he was the first to admit the challenges an entrepreneur's perspective can bring to a growing business, Sam was also quick to see the danger of losing creative influence, vision, and relationship with the associates.

Management brought in a woman VP of Sales, who immediately took control of everything Sam had been doing in marketing. Her style of management did nothing for the morale of the employees, and complaints began to pile up. Sam had managed to retain his title as President of the company, but his authority was rapidly diminishing.

During this same time we went on an Alaskan cruise with leading Mannatech distributors and our corporate executives. While on this cruise that I had a chance to talk to the CEO on a personal level. I prayed before I talked to him because I felt that the Lord had a message for him. He and his wife were very forthright, and we had a good, open discussion. I gave him the history of Mannatech and included the spiritual component attached to it. I told him that Mannatech was a gift from the Lord, and we all had to be very careful not to abuse it. I remember telling him that we all had special talents, which God wanted us to use to contribute to the success of Mannatech, and we were not very effective if we operated outside of our gifting. I was frank with him about what I saw as his lack of appreciation for Sam's talents. He was obviously a bit shocked at my boldness as was Sam when I told him of my conversation.

Things really did not change much for a while. Our prayer group continued to pray for Ron to see his position at Mannatech as a blessing. We prayed for his heart to change and for God's perfect will in the situation. In March of 1998, Mannatech had an event in Calgary, Canada. I was in the back of the room praying during the whole event, (I often feel God leads me to pray at key times). While the CEO was on stage speaking, the Lord impressed on me very clearly that he would be gone in April. (I believe that God gives all of us many opportunities to come into alignment with his purposes in order to bless us, but He will never force His will on us. However, if we continue to oppose Him I believe He will remove us from that blessing.)

When we got home, I told my prayer group about it, and we continued to pray for Ron. March came and went. We were well into April, and there was no indication that Ron was leaving, but I knew deep in my spirit what the Lord had shown me. By this time, the new VP of Sales had alienated many of the top associates, most of our vendors, and all of the marketing employees. Ron had lost complete control of her and of our IT department as well. Sam was so upset with the situation that he called a meeting with Skip and

Bill. Sam explained the seriousness of the state of the business, and all three decided that a major change needed to occur.

On April 30th, Sam called me from the office and told me that Ron had been asked to resign and the VP of Sales had been let go. Both left with large financial settlements, a precedent that would one day cost Mannatech millions of dollars in similar terminations. Skip immediately took over as "interim" CEO. Once again, I felt a strong spiritual opposition to this decision, but Sam agreed with it since Skip and Bill had supported him on both of the recent management changes. Sam's optimism was short-lived. A new agenda would soon arise that would be the biggest turning point in the company's history—going public!

Chapter Eleven

Going Public—
A Titanic Event

Skip and Sam made a real attempt to work with each other, but their agendas were so diametrically opposed that it was a very challenging situation. I assumed, at the time, that Skip had a sincere appreciation for Sam's talents, and Sam appreciated Skip's willingness to try to make things work. Both wanted the company to succeed, but for different reasons. Skip wanted the personal, financial rewards, and Sam wanted to fulfill the vision. The two agendas were destined to clash. To Skip's credit, he was totally honest and forthright about his goals. He never pretended to be in it for a greater cause; he was there to make money.

As Mannatech grew, the new corporate attorney began to tighten the reigns on our associates' activities. Her marching orders were to eliminate potential legal risks stemming from corporate marketing materials, personal testimonials or advertising by our associates. This was done in order to protect the company's "cash flow." Unfortunately, this new regulatory environment began to bring marketing to a standstill and to severely restrict the associates' business building strategies—the very strategies that had built the company. Volume in North America began to flatten out. Cash became tighter, and a new strategy would need to be implemented to continue the executive wealth building. The answer—going public.

From the very day that Sam told me the Board of Directors had decided to take the company public, I felt strongly it was a bad decision. I wasn't exactly sure why I felt that way, but I knew it was a feeling deep in my spirit. I could rationalize in my head all the reasons why not: we could be much more scrutinized, the potential for a larger company to merge or buy us out would be greater, there was the possibility for turning the company away from network marketing; but I was sure there was a more significant reason. Could we be going against the will of God? In my opinion, nothing was worth that.

I prayed and fasted (and quite frankly, I agonized over the decision). But things moved full steam ahead to take Mannatech public. Sam felt like he was between a rock and a hard place. He understood the board's proposal, but he also knew there was something very real about what I felt.

At the next board meeting, they voted that the top-level executives should all be offered employment contracts. That was not at all unusual for a company that was going public. In fact, according to the experts, it is often recommended. The details were yet to be worked out. A few weeks later, Sam and five other executives were handed their contracts. When Sam read the terms, he was appalled.

The contracts were approved for five years with an automatic one-year renewal clause at the end of each year. That meant that if the executive were demoted or ever asked to leave, the company would have to pay him/her a severance of five years salary plus all benefits and stock options.

Sam refused to sign his contract on the basis that he felt it was unfair to future stock holders. These contracts, in effect, would strap the company with about eighteen million dollars worth of never-ending debt. Sam discussed his concern with another executive who was also receiving a contract. The executive agreed that while it was certainly generous, it was also perfectly legal for a private company to issue contracts to its executive team. Besides, he explained, this was his security for the future. He was surprised by Sam's refusal to sign his contract and asked how he could feel so secure without one. Sam answered that he trusted in God to provide his every need and that he could never, with integrity, face a future stockholder if he signed that contract. The executive just commented on how strange Sam was and then left. Sam became the only top executive without a contract.

It took several months to enlist a banking firm to underwrite the public offering, and there were several false starts. Each time there was a delay, it reinforced my belief that we should not go public, but finally the deal got put together and the "road show" began. [A road show is when company executives travel with their bankers to major cities in the country to "sell" large institutional investors on their IPO (initial public offering) of stock.]

In a month's time, Sam, Skip, and Pat, the CFO, traveled to four or five cities a week. The proposed purpose for going public was to raise the money to expand internationally. Mannatech had grown to annual sales of $165 million in North America in just five years, and the timing seemed right. Sam said the investors, overall, were impressed with the company, with the exception of two things. First, a large portion of the company's profits had been given to the owners as bonuses. Second, sales were flattening out in North America. Logical reasons were given for both and the investors seemed satisfied.

My feelings about going public only intensified with time. I believed, with everything in me, that this was the wrong decision. I asked God for some reassurance, and immediately the scripture that came to my mind was Mark 11:22-24. Jesus said, *"Have faith in God. Truly I say to you, whoever says to this mountain, 'Be taken up and cast into the sea,' and does NOT DOUBT in his heart, but believes that what he says is going to happen, it will be granted him. Therefore I say to you, all things for which you pray and ask, believe that you have received them, and they will be granted you."* I felt God was telling me that I was going to need a lot of faith for what was ahead. That was an understatement!

Iceberg Ahead!

A few days later on June 9th, 1998, I turned on the television, and a pastor was giving a sermon on the Mark 11:22-24 scripture. I went out to my patio and prayed. I wanted confirmation on what the Lord was telling me. As I began to pray, a very realistic picture or impression came to my mind. I was on a huge ship, like a cruise ship, and in the front of it was a Mannatech flag. We were on a vast ocean, and far ahead of us was an iceberg with the letters IPO. I knew that they stood for Initial Public Offering. The Lord told me to quote the Mark 11:22-24 scripture, and as I did, the iceberg sank into the ocean.

From that point on, I was confident that the IPO would not happen. I can't explain the sense of finality I had, but the reality of God's power was unbelievable! It's these types of encounters with the Lord that, on one hand, humble me, but, on the other hand, strengthen me. When I told Sam about what God had shown me, he was amazed. I told him that he might as well come home because there was no way the company was going public. He understood what I was saying and said he believed I was hearing from the Lord, but he thought he should finish the road show. Sam said that the bankers were very positive about the offering, but he also knew that God could stop it any time. I couldn't understand his thinking. If he felt as I had, then why not just come home?

I was spending quite a bit of time in prayer now. As I did, God would lead me to story after story in the Bible, which continued to confirm His plans for Mannatech. I prayed for many other things also, but this seemed to be a season where God wanted me to focus most of my prayer time on Mannatech. I prayed for God to give wisdom to Sam and the board, I prayed for humility for everyone in the company, and I prayed for all associates to prosper in all their ways. The more I prayed, the more I was comforted.

Clarity—The Long Awaited Gift

On July 13th, 1998, I left for Edmonton, Canada, to go to Mannatech's Canadian National Event. Although there was still no final approval from the SEC for the IPO, Sam was on the road show that week and was planning to meet me in Canada in a few days. While I was there, I got together with some very good friends, Colin and Lynette Ruttle. I shared with them the whole IPO matter and how Sam and I had differing views on the issue. We began to pray, and as we did, Lynette said, "Linda, the Lord has purposely kept Sam from seeing what you see so that he can stay focused on what he was called to do. As you pray, you lay a pathway for Sam, brick by brick, so that he has clear direction. In God's time, He'll give Sam the wisdom to carry out His plan."

That was a huge revelation! It was the piece of the puzzle that had been missing. I instantly realized that every time I got a word or impression from God, I expected Sam to act on it immediately. That was when the pressure would always come. I was placing my expectations on Sam, therefore not trusting in God. I now knew my only job was to give Sam the information God had revealed. His job was to implement it as God led.

Lynette helped me fully see that God has given Sam a gift of wisdom. He knows when and how to take action. Sam had not been saying that he didn't believe me about the IPO; he was simply saying that coming home was not the wise thing for him to do. This was a pivotal point in our lives. From that day forward, I was able to give Sam any insight I received and then let it go. There was so much freedom in the fact that I no longer had to put my expectations on him. Sam trusted me when I said I got a directive from God, and I trusted him to act on it at the appropriate time. This revelation brought tremendous healing into our relationship and allowed us to work with each other instead of against each other. (Thank you Lynette, for that significant insight and for your friendship.)

Thursday Sam flew into Edmonton. He only had about 20 minutes on stage before he had to leave to rejoin the road show group in Colorado. Since there was so much interest in the IPO, he gave everyone an update. Later that night and throughout the weekend several people told me that they did not have a good feeling about the company going public. It was obvious to me that the conflict over this issue was heating up.

The following Tuesday, I left Edmonton to go back home to Dallas. Sam called me from Houston and said that they finally got approval from the SEC for an initial public offering. Sam said the bankers were thrilled with the news and with the response they were getting back from the investor groups. I thought, "Well, this will be interesting to see how God works this out. Mannatech got man's approval for the IPO, but they don't have God's approval." I knew the Lord was going to do something miraculous; He was going to surprise us all.

The IPO was supposed to be finalized on Friday, July 31st, in New York City. I decided that I would fast and pray for the last three days. I called Lydia, Colin and Lynette, and some other prayer partners to pray with me. I asked the Lord to show me a scripture that would encourage me. I could not believe my eyes when I opened the Bible to Habakkuk 1:5! It said, *"...Watch and be utterly amazed! For I am going to do something in your days that you would not believe, even if you were told."* (New International Version) I thanked God for being so faithful and encouraging.

No Surprise Here

On Wednesday, July 29th, I woke up with such a peace in my heart. My children and I had a great day together, riding horses and talking about all kinds of things. They asked about the IPO and when Sam would be home. I said, "He's supposed to come home Friday, but let's pray that he'll be home tomorrow." About 7:30 p.m. Sam called from New York City and said, "Everyone here is in shock because the IPO did not go through!" He said that early that day everything looked good, but later in the day the market had taken a big drop and the investors got nervous. By 5:00 p.m., the deadline for "booking" the offering, there weren't enough commitments to complete the deal.

The bankers immediately implemented a contingency plan. They would drop the offering amount and try to book the offering the following week with the commitments they had received. It would still give Mannatech all the cash it needed to expand and would be just a slight detour from the original plan. Sam spoke up and voted against it. The offering had failed; it was over.

In previous years, Sam might have gone along with the contingency plan because it seemed logical, but now he and I and the Lord were working together. God showed me the plan, I told Sam, and he acted on it when the time was right. Lynette was right in how our gifts worked. Sam said he would be home the next day, and I immediately called all my prayer partners and shared the miracle. We thanked God for His faithfulness and celebrated the victory.

This incident catapulted Sam into a new level of faith. We discussed the events of the past few months and continued to be in awe at God's hand in the whole situation. We marveled at our newfound "partnership." Now we were not only partners in marriage, we were partners in business. In retrospect, we had to get to this point in order for God to use us in the future for what He had planned.

Things at Mannatech got back to normal for Sam, which was not always a good thing. Again his hands were tied because of the lack of understanding about network marketing on the part of his partners and the Board of Directors. Sam felt that God wanted us to do much more with the gift of Ambrotose, but he wasn't sure how to proceed with the current management. We prayed and asked God for wisdom and understanding. It was out of this prayer that the next phase of our Joseph calling was birthed.

Chapter Twelve

To Whom Much Is Given

It was November 1998, and Sam and I were driving and discussing different business issues. Almost out of nowhere, Sam said that we should start a non-profit organization and send our products to orphanages. Sam, on his own, had already been sending Phyto-Bears to orphanages in Romania through a friend of his named Judy Broom. Judy started an organization called Hug International and had personally seen the tremendous need to help those children on many different levels. She was amazed at the difference the Phyto-Bears made in their lives in just a few weeks. In fact, that first winter they had less illness and no deaths from disease for the first time in all the years she had been working in Romania.

We began tossing around different names for the new company and came up with MannaRelief. Never having been involved with non-profits or ministries before, we knew if it were going to succeed, that God would have to walk us through it. We asked Don and Lydia to be on our Board of Directors, and we asked Dr. Reg McDaniel if we could rent a small space from a non-profit organization he worked with called The Fisher Institute. He welcomed us, and we took off from there. In the beginning all funds came from the four of us on the board, but it wasn't long before the associates jumped in and began helping MannaRelief as well.

Sam had a new surge of hope and energy because of what we saw through MannaRelief. His heart had always been to help people, especially children, but he also realized that the business model of Mannatech would pass up millions of children in North America and around the world who could benefit from our products. Through his years of experience with nutrition companies, Sam had seen that the parents of chronically ill children often became physically, emotionally, financially, and spiritually bankrupt searching for options for their dying children. MannaRelief provided the best way to touch these families. Because of our domestic and international giving, Sam could now see a tangible way of becoming a company of provision to a hurting world.

Clashing Agendas

He was so thrilled about the opportunity that he presented the plan to Mannatech's executive team. But instead of being excited, they raised several objections. First, if MannaRelief gave product away, wouldn't that conceivably take away from potential company profits? Sam tried to explain that giving in this way would only bless the company. Second, wouldn't there be a potential loss of business for the associates? Sam said that our associates would never feel threatened by helping orphans or chronically ill children and besides the program would only work with their involvement. Other objections surfaced, but no decision was made until the next board meeting.

The subject had obviously been discussed with the board members prior to the next meeting because when the subject came up everyone was ready. First, the attorney warned the directors of all the potential legal challenges, which could surface if the company was involved with a charity. Second, the issue of potential lost revenue was discussed. Skip then declared that as long as he had a controlling stock position, Mannatech would never become involved with anything like MannaRelief. All other board members went along.

Their one concession was that they would make product available to Sam at cost if he wanted to pursue this on his own, but no one in the company would be allowed to help in any way. It was made clear to Sam that if he solicited the help of any employee, that employee's job would be in jeopardy.

When Sam shared the Board's position with Lydia, Don, and myself, we were disappointed but not shocked. We all agreed that MannaRelief reflected the heart of God, and honestly believed nothing would stop it from moving forward. In a way it was actually better to be separated from the company. As an extension of our faith, we launched MannaRelief as a ministry of provision to sick and hurting children of all races, of all faiths, and in all countries. We were free to pray for and offer support to the children in any way we deemed necessary.

MannaRelief was launched and Mannatech's Board of Directors could not have been more wrong about the associates' attitude towards us. They not only overwhelmingly supported the children's programs; they also contributed the majority of the money needed to begin touching thousands of children around the world. By their actions the associates confirmed to us that they are people with tremendous hearts.

The Gift of Grace

On December 24, 1998, we adopted our third child. Grace Ann Caster was born on December 22, and she was the perfect Christmas gift for our family. Like her big sister Hannah, she had brown hair and was absolutely precious. The whole family went to the hospital to pick her up, and then we went to church to celebrate the birth of Jesus and to thank Him for the birth of our daughter. Sam and I felt very blessed in every area of our lives.

Sam was often kept in the dark concerning things of a corporate nature. One day during my prayer time, the Lord strongly impressed on me that the Board of Directors was going to get rid of Sam. I didn't share that with anyone else but Sam. (There are times when I believe the Lord wants me to keep things to myself until He directs me otherwise). Sam said there was no way they would get rid of him. "I don't get in the way of anything they want to do. All I want is to make Mannatech the best company ever, and I'm willing to do whatever it takes, so why would they want to get rid of me?" I told him that God did not reveal to me the "whys," but He wanted us to be aware that there was a plan in action.

Going Public—Round Two

Mannatech executives were determined to find a way to take the company public. They decided that instead of going to institutional buyers, they would go to the associates and have a "directed public offering." (A directed public offering is an offering of company stock to one particular group.) After what happened with the IPO Sam was not as convinced as the other executives that this was the direction to take, but he did feel that making an offer to the associates was different from selling it first to Wall Street. I, on the other hand, adhered to my belief that Mannatech should not go public under any circumstance.

Management announced they were going to do a road show to present the new offering to the associates. They asked Sam to go with them but he said he'd rather not. He didn't want to influence the associates to do something he himself was unsure of. Sam thought if it wasn't supposed to happen it wouldn't, but he did not feel he should attempt to stop it.

Mannatech had to raise a minimum of twenty million dollars by February 12, 1999, in order to go public. The offering price was eight dollars per share. By February 11th, Mannatech had a commitment from associates to purchase twenty-four million dollars of stock.

This time I was the one who was shocked! I didn't understand why this had happened. Why had God stopped it the first time but not the second? So many questions went through my mind. I became weary emotionally and spiritually. I didn't want to think about Mannatech any more, much less pray for it. I felt this way for the rest of that year and redirected my focus to MannaRelief.

The same weekend the company went public was also our national convention in Dallas, but I had no desire to attend. Jett, one of our top associates, received the Distributor of the Year trophy, but he gave it to Sam because he said that Sam had been such an encouragement to him. From the stage that night, Jett gave Sam a check for MannaRelief in the amount of twenty thousand dollars and encouraged Ray Robbins and the Presidentials in the company to give also. We were so thankful for the generous way in which they responded. MannaRelief was able to send product to so many more children that year than we had hoped for.

Locked Up And Dumped

For the first six months after the company went public, all insiders, (those of us who had original stock), were to be locked up. That meant we were prohibited from selling stock during that time. However, when management rewrote new offering documents, three top executives lock-up period was changed from the original six months to only ninety days.

The day that Mannatech stock opened on NASDAQ as MTEX, it went up to over twenty dollars per share. The second day it went up to over forty dollars per share! A reporting agency stated that day traders thought Mannatech was an Internet stock, which at the time always created a feeding frenzy. When the day traders figured out their mistake and sold, the stock price dropped back to around eighteen dollars per share and stayed there for the next three months.

After the first ninety days the stock began to take a dip. Trading was suddenly excessive. The three top executives who had received the ninety-day lock-up period, were selling their shares in massive volumes. The associates began calling and asking Sam why insiders were dumping their stock. Sam had no idea what they were talking about. He was under the false impression that all insiders were locked up for six months. When he asked about it, Sam was told they were sorry if he did not understand that the rules had been changed for those three executives, but it was disclosed in the offering documents. Sam had even signed off on those documents without actually reading the fine print because he trustingly assumed everything was just as they had agreed to in the first offering.

But beyond the misunderstanding of the lockup period, the bigger issue was the amount of stock being dumped on the market at one time. Millions of dollars of stock were sold in just a thirty-day period, causing the price to plummet. I had never seen Sam so mad. Sales were flat, insiders were driving down the value of the stock through their selling, and a hiring and promotion freeze was implemented on the employees.

In the midst of this turmoil, the Board of Directors decided to lease a private jet to take them to the Bahamas for a board meeting. When Sam got the memo, he immediately delivered a letter to the executive team and the board, asserting his frustration with their lack of sensitivity to what was happening to the company. He refused to go to the board meeting in the Bahamas or any other meetings of that nature. The chasm between Sam and the board was becoming increasingly wide, and neither side was about to budge.

In our home school classroom, I have a large banner that reads, **"Stand Up For What Is Right, Even If You Stand Alone."** Sam was becoming the embodiment of that powerful phrase right before my very eyes. I was so proud of him for taking this stance. For a person who hates conflict, he had ventured way outside of his comfort zone.

One of the company executives called Sam to try to change his mind. It happened to be one of the insiders who was dumping stock. When Sam confronted this person on the selling of stock, the individual explained that it was their way of securing their financial future. Sam asked what he thought their dumping was doing to the attitude of our shareholders, our associates. "How are the associates supposed to promote confidence in our company when our own executives are obviously 'cashing out'?" Sam asked. The only answer he got was "We're not doing anything illegal."

The next day the board left for the Bahamas without Sam. He was later told that it was at the meeting in the Bahamas, that unofficially, the discussions began in reference to removing him from Mannatech. Neither Sam nor I knew it at the time, although we probably could have guessed if we had thought about it, that my previous revelation of his being fired was going into effect that weekend. Sam had become a true outsider to the insiders.

As much as I appreciated Sam's new boldness, I could not help but believe that we were now paying for his initial lack of discernment in the founding of the company. I knew with all my heart that God's grace was still on the company and on Sam. As bad as things seemed, I felt Sam's recent decisions had initiated a turn for the best in the spiritual realm. I was actually excited about what was to come. I knew God could really use Sam now, like never before, but I had no idea how God was about to test Sam. Again, as I look back on that time, I can see that Sam had only passed "Faith Building 101." Graduate school was about to begin.

Chapter Thirteen

Death Of A Dream

When the six-month lockup ended, stock selling escalated again. Bill Fioretti, who was no longer with the company, had close to five million shares that he desperately wanted to sell. Skip, as well as some other insiders, also sold various numbers of shares. Over the next year the stock price continued to fall and finally hit a low in the ninety-cent per share range. Mannatech received bad press and the associates were discouraged by all the self-inflicted wounds that management kept imposing on the company.

Concurrently, a Mannatech executive came up with the idea of selling generic nutritional products on a web site they named "Clickwell." The goal was to capture some business from the associate base, as well as from the Internet market. Sam tried to explain that if there were not a commission structure for associates, there would be little or no business. Other executives were convinced that anything on the Internet would translate to instant success; therefore, they didn't believe they needed the associates' business. Immediately after the company launched this multi-million-dollar project, the bottom fell out of the Internet industry. Clickwell was a financial disaster, as well as another PR blunder for the company.

Also taking place at this time was the opening of Mannatech in the United Kingdom. Sam and I spoke from stage at the opening event. We shared our faith and the calling we felt God had placed on the company. Our statements were very well received, however one visitor in attendance complained to management that it was inappropriate to talk about one's faith at a business meeting. After the event some senior executives told Sam that they were unhappy with our comments and vowed not to let Sam take part in the international market again.

Sam's separation from the executive team became more and more obvious. I prayed that if the company had to crash to get back on track with God's purpose, then let it crash. I know that may sound drastic to some people, but, honestly, I felt it was similar to my praying for my brother. I saw Mannatech spiritually as a lost child who had abandoned God for its own pleasure, and as I had done for my brother, I asked God to do whatever necessary to get its attention. My prayers were answered almost immediately.

In May of 2000, Skip Fioretti began talking to Sam about stepping down as CEO so that he could focus more of his time on his Chairman of the Board position. (Although, he wanted to retain his full salary and benefits.) Skip told Sam that he had spoken to other board members about hiring a former consultant named Bob Henry as the new CEO and if he agreed they would proceed. Sam was so pleased with Skip's decision to relinquish the CEO position that he agreed on the spot.

Bob Henry had previously worked for Avon and had a financial background in the direct sales industry. He had also been a consultant with an investment firm called the Gryphon Group who had come to Mannatech months earlier with a proposal to purchase the majority position in the company. They needed Sam's and my stock to make the deal work, but we were adamantly opposed to the offer so nothing ever came of it.

Sam eagerly called me and said to call Don and Lydia to meet us at Starbucks to talk about the latest series of events at Mannatech. As Sam told us about Skips' decision to step down, we were all elated, but as he shared the rest of the story, that familiar feeling of nausea came over me. As soon as Sam mentioned the name Bob Henry I knew in my spirit that something was very wrong. I had never met Bob, so it was not personal, but I knew God was warning me to watch and pray. My reaction to Bob was a shock to Sam because we had been praying for so long for someone else to step in as CEO.

Needless to say, the celebration that Sam had anticipated at Starbucks came to an abrupt halt. It was too late for Sam to change his mind. The decision had already been made to hire Bob. At that very moment, I felt things had shifted spiritually and that things concerning the direction of Mannatech would get worse before they got better. That turned out to be the prophetic understatement of the year.

Fired—Promoted—Resigned

On a Friday, April 5, 2000, when Sam came home, I could tell by the heaviness on him that something awful had happened. It was late that night when he sat me down and told me there had been a board meeting that day, and the Board of Directors voted to remove (fire) him as president of the company. The board had a long discussion about it, and everyone gave their reasons why, but, clearly, the decision had been made before the meeting even started. The board members said, that, in order to be a "real" public company and to expand internationally, they needed to put the right people in the right positions. Sam was told that he did not have the skills for his position and that he was going to be "promoted" to co-chairman of the board with Skip, who was officially stepping down as CEO.

The decision had been made to put Terry Persinger, a former top executive with Goodyear, now Mannatech's COO and board member, in the position of President. Bob Henry was voted in as the new CEO.

In Sam's heart, he knew the move had been calculated to finally remove him from any position of authority. God's earlier revelation to me was unfolding before our very eyes. The spiritual battle was mounting. It was a battle between light and darkness, between God's will and Satan's will. Ultimately, it was a battle for the fulfillment of God's vision for Mannatech and us.

Sam had argued with the board for hours, but to no avail. Only four votes were required to move Sam out, and those four had obviously been decided before discussions began. Later, one of the four told Sam that he didn't believe it was the right decision to remove him, but he felt loyal to the group for all the money he had made. The board told Sam that the change would go smoothly in the field if he would just get behind it and support it.

Oddly enough, I felt that this was the answer to my prayers. This was positively going to be the catalyst that would lead to the ultimate goal of getting the company back into our hands so God could direct His plan through us. Sam and I, once again, were in complete agreement.

The next month was a whirlwind of events. Sam left the board meeting with mixed emotions. He had no idea what to do next. He informed management that he was going to take a couple of weeks off to think about his options. The changing of Sam's position was announced to the associate leaders the following Monday. On the surface it seemed like a good move. Bob Henry and Terry Persinger seemed like qualified executives to take on the roles of CEO and President, and Sam had supposedly been "elevated" to co-chairman.

You Can Fool The Fans, But Not The Players

However, there was one thing the board had underestimated. Some associate leaders, like Don Partridge, Dwight and Susan Havener, Peter and Anita Robutka, and Ray Gebauer knew instinctively that something wrong and they wanted to know what it was. Sam had always kept an open line of communication with them and they knew he would never voluntarily step down without first having explained it to the field leadership. This was an incredibly uncomfortable position for Terry Persinger and Bob Henry, but they were caught in the middle of a huge battle that had only just begun. Since this battle was spiritually based, it was outside the scope of normal understanding.

Sam and I fasted and prayed. We knew that although things were out of our hands, they were still in the hands of God. We met with our prayer group regularly. We all believed that, in spite of the way things looked, God was up to something great. Sam's first move was to go back to Skip and talk candidly and honestly about his feelings. He told Skip that if the purpose of the board was to put the right people in the right place, then Sam's position should be chairman of the board, not co-chairman with Skip.

He and Skip talked frankly about each other's agendas and expectations from the business. Skip, as usual, was open, but not in agreement. He said that he would take the proposal to the board for discussion. Skip and Sam, by the way, never argued or had harsh words with each other; they simply saw things from completely different perspectives.

Skip immediately reported back to Sam that there would be no deal. But he also told Sam that if he could find a buyer for his stock he would sell out and leave the company. Sam told Skip that he would go to work on that. Sam's top priority then became that of finding the right person to purchase Skip's stock.

In the meantime, things were heating up at corporate. Bob Henry was ready to get on with his new role as CEO. He was becoming frustrated with Sam for being out of the office and challenged, I'm sure, by the uncertainty of the events that were unfolding day by day. On May 2, 2000, Bob sent Sam a letter requesting his immediate return. Finding a buyer for Skip was not going to happen fast, if at all. What Sam was to do next, however, was the decision of a lifetime.

Sam was perplexed. On the one hand, he knew he could make everything "appear" to be okay if he just returned to the office. He agonized over the distraction this entire mess was causing in the field. Competitors would have a field day with the situation. Sam had such a personal attachment to the associates that his first instinct was to spare them any more grief. On the other hand, there was no way he could lie to the associates about the reality of what was happening. Sam and I prayed and fasted for God's guidance, but there was no clear answer.

An Answer From Abraham

One day while I was praying, I thought about the story of Abraham and Isaac. The story, which is in Genesis, chapter 22, tells of Abraham's devotion and faith to God, no matter His command. Long before this chapter, God had promised Abraham and Sarah a son and through that son, a nation. They waited so long for their son, that at times they doubted God's promise. Finally, the long-awaited day came, Isaac was born, and he was the apple of his parent's eye.

Years later, God told Abraham to take his son to a nearby mountaintop and sacrifice him there. Abraham courageously obeyed the Lord. He took Isaac and two other men with him, and on the third day he found the mountain. Abraham built an altar and placed Isaac on it. He then stretched out his hand and took the knife to slay his son. At that very moment, the angel of the Lord called to Abraham (in Genesis 22:12) and said, *"Do not stretch out your hand against the lad, and do nothing to him; for now I know that you fear God, since you have not withheld your son, your only son, from Me."* Abraham then turned his eyes to look, and there behind him was a ram caught in a thicket by its horns. So Abraham took the ram and offered it to the Lord. Abraham called the name of the place *"The Lord Will Provide."*

As I thought of this story, it seemed analogous to Sam and Mannatech. Mannatech was birthed from the heart of God, who then placed it in the heart of Sam. Sam loved the company and the associates. In spite of all the adverse circumstances, he saw the good in Mannatech. He felt a responsibility and a burden to nurture it and to make sure everyone involved had the best opportunity to succeed. I was certain that the Lord was now asking Sam, just as he had Abraham and my brother-in-law Don, *"Do you trust Me no matter what? Do you believe if I ask you to lay down the thing you love that I will provide a ram in the thicket?"* It appeared that Sam had come to a fork in the road, and he was going to have to make a huge decision. In retrospect, this situation was much more about Sam's relationship with the Lord and with me than it was about Mannatech. In God's infinite wisdom, He knew that in order for Mannatech to move forward in the way He wanted it to, there was going to have to be a heart change in both Sam and me.

For the most part, when it came to business, Sam and I had rarely been in unity spiritually. That had all changed. We now knew, without a doubt, what we needed to do. We were thrust into the place where God had wanted us all along. The process of seeking the Lord together drew us closer in our marriage. As a result, Sam and I opened up to one another and shared things that we hadn't talked about before. God was purging us from everything that kept us from having a full, complete relationship with Him and with each other. It was the best thing that ever happened to us.

We made a commitment to pray and fast together for three days to find the next step God wanted us to take. At the end of the fast, which was on May 3, 2000, we woke up and asked one another if we felt a strong leaning toward what to do. Sam said that he felt he was supposed to resign from the Board of Directors. He said that he could not, in good faith, support that group any more. I completely agreed with him, and, with that, he took that huge step of faith and laid down the company he loved.

Sam wrote his resignation letter (see page 86), and we gathered our children and prayed. He then faxed the letter to the board members and it was over. As difficult as that was for Sam, we knew it was the right thing to do. Once again I was so proud of his stand and his faith in God.

As mentioned in his resignation letter, Sam also wrote and faxed to the board a proposal for changes in the company leadership that he wanted to see take place. The proposal called for an immediate change of certain board members, a company buy-out of Skip and Bill's remaining stock, and the renegotiations of all senior management's revolving five-year contracts. This proposal, of course, was refused. Next Sam sent a letter to the associate leaders with a copy of his resignation letter (see page 87).

Since Sam had never signed a contract, he had no severance package. According to the company by-laws, he was prohibited from starting another company for one year. We had promised the associates that we would never sell our stock for less than eight-dollars-per-share, the price at which it had opened, and we intended to keep that promise. So Sam left Mannatech with nothing but his integrity, which for us was more than enough. It was the beginning of a new walk of faith in God, but we were filled with a reassuring peace.

Because the company was publicly owned, they had to put out a press release announcing Sam's resignation. From that moment, we were inundated with phone calls. People were absolutely dumfounded. Over the years, Sam and I had kept most of what went on inside the company quiet. We felt it was best not to disrupt the field with negative information.

Sam told the associates that his heart would always be with Mannatech and that as a major shareholder, he would do whatever he could to help the company. But, for now, Sam felt that he would serve them best from the outside. Sam and I could certainly empathize with them because our hearts were as broken as theirs were.

The love and encouragement we received from the field was overwhelming. I know it was their support that, in large part, helped us through this difficult time. Following is a sampling of literally hundreds of e-mails we received.

Sam and Linda, along with so many thousands of others, you are very important to Gloria and me. Regardless of position or status, I believe the anointing of the Lord is on you to give guidance to Mannatech Inc.
—Eugene Fox

Our prayers are with you as we support you 100%. Remember you have the strength of a committed army to draw upon. We are prepared to stand by you NO MATTER WHAT.
May God Bless Your Efforts,
—Marshall, Brenda, Austin, and Ashton Howard

We fully believe in you and your leadership. Our confidence and peace comes from knowing that you are seeking God's guidance. Blessings and Love,

—Tony and Rheta Buoy-Somohano
We unite with you and stand in faith believing that NO MAN can bring down the hand of God!
—George and Margaret Dubouch

I am joining you today in prayer and fasting for God's will to be made known and I am confident you will hear His voice. We love you guys.
—Bette and Don Kitt

Our prayers are with you and Sam and all the people who care about the mission of Mannatech. Blessings,
—Noni (Kaufman), David (Lawlor), and Isabella

Lori and I want to express our love for you both and our prayers are with you. We believe God is in control and he will use you both to put Mannatech where we belong. God's Blessings.
—Gary Puckett

Sam and Linda, you are the heart of Mannatech. We are trusting absolutely that the future of Mannatech is in the hands of God and that you and Sam will be an even more important part of it.
In His Love,
—Maria Elliott

God is in control of everything. We want you to know that our prayers are with you and your children. We are 100% behind both of you. You both are such an inspiration to us.
    –Ken and Dottie Anderson

Be assured of our prayers for guidance and for a willing heart all to be changed. Do not be discouraged.
    –Peggy and Ted Bendell

Thank you for your willingness to uphold solid moral and ethical principles in behalf of Mannatech. You are in our prayers daily.
    –Dick and Yvonne McDaniel

I am wholeheartedly behind you and Sam. You can count on me 100%. Much Love,
    –Marcia Smith

I am proud of how you are handling all this. I am glad to be a part of your vision.
    –Carol Merlo

We are 100% behind you. We really do love you guys and will do whatever we can to help.
    –Fred and Denise Vance

Sam's removal as President and resignation from the board caused so much disruption in the field that the company was forced to intervene. Bob Henry requested a proposal from Sam for his immediate return to the company. Sam and I prayed and then met with our attorney concerning the terms of his return. Sam was uncompromising as he responded with a letter outlining the same basic conditions as his first proposal. The proposal was quickly rejected. Since Sam so boldly called for the removal of certain board members and the renegotiations of those five-year contracts, he felt the only way he would be able to return was to find a buyer for Skip and Bill Fioretti's stock. With the present state of the company, that seemed impossible, but we could see no other way.

Sam and I put everything on the line and put our complete trust in God. We prayed for direction, and in just two week's the answer came. It was the farthest thing from what either one of us thought it would be.

May 3, 2000

TO: Robert M. Henry, Chief Executive Officer, Terry L. Persinger, President and Chief
        Operating Officer, and to the other members of the Board of Directors of Mannatech
        Incorporated:

This letter is to give you notice that I am resigning as a director, officer and employee of the
Company and its subsidiaries, effective immediately.

Due to the recent decision to remove me as President of Mannatech, Inc. and the subsequent refusal
(according to Skip Fioretti) of certain board members to consider promoting me to Chairman of the
Board, I no longer feel empowered to make a significant contribution to this Company. This decision has come after weeks of prayer and soul searching. I now feel that our business philosophies
are irreconcilable in light of these actions.

I am sending a proposal for your consideration that contains an offer to Skip and Bill for the
Company's purchase of their stock and to resolve many long-term contract issues. If accepted by
all concerned parties, I would love to once again devote my full time efforts in the building of this
Company. I am making this last effort because both Bill and Skip have expressed on numerous
occasions their desire to cash out and leave the Company. This may accomplish everyone's goals,
as my desire has always been to stay and build. I trust that everyone is doing what they feel is best
for the Company. I respectfully offer this proposal as my best resolution.

If the board declines to follow my recommendation, I wish you success as I am still a major stockholder in this Company. I would encourage you to consider that, in my opinion, our biggest hurdle
in the field is the destroyed confidence that our associates have in our corporate management due to
insider stock selling. As I have stated on numerous occasions, we are in a relationship business. It
is not about products, science, great-looking management or earnings per share that builds this business. It is the trust from our associates in our vision that moves people into action. This trust has
been eroded and you must get it back. No marketing campaign, Japan opening, or product rollout
will ever trigger growth — only trust will do that.

Sincerely,

Sam Caster

Sam Caster

Subj: **Dear Associates: From Sam Caster**
Date: 05/07/2000
From: Lindacaster

Dear Associates,

I am writing this short note to give some explanation to my recent decision to resign from the Board of Mannatech. Please see my attached resignation letter that sheds some light on the chain of events that led to my decision.

I believe that Mannatech is at a crossroads, a crossroads of philosophy, agendas, and direction. I am not claiming to have all of the answers to the challenges of building this company but I know that my vision, my feel for the needs of our associates, and my authority to provide balance and perspective to those who are focused mainly on Wall Street's view of us is an absolute necessity. When I was voted out of my position of authority and refused to vote on chairman, I knew that a major shift in power had occurred, a move that I could not embrace nor promote in good faith. I have seen our company shift from an environment of openness and excitement to one of control and bottom line. Legal and regulatory have become "weapons" of control over market-ing and associate strategies, while establishing power bases for a few self-serving agendas. Instead of facing and dealing with the real problems that have been stifling growth in our current markets there is an overwhelming view from many that opening in Japan will fix everything, it won't. It will magnify our challenges times ten.

I am through defending and making excuses for those in Mannatech whose personal agendas are always being put above the good of our associates. I am going to fight for this company. I resigned from the board to enable me to do this more effectively, but please don't confuse the word resign with quit, I'm not discouraged, I'm con-victed. Mannatech is the greatest company in the world; I'm just tired of seeing it abused. For me, it's all or nothing.

Sincerely,

Sam Caster

Chapter Fourteen

The Road To San Antonio Experience

In mid-May, 2000, there was a Mannatech event in Orlando, Florida which we did not attend since Sam no longer worked for the company. The top associates met with Skip Fioretti, Bob Henry, and Terry Persinger, to discuss the company's future and the possibility of Sam's return. We received one phone call after another asking Sam to come to Orlando to help resolve the issues. Sam and I decided that nothing would be gained by our going, so we loaded up the car with our children and went to San Antonio for some much needed R&R, and to get away from the phones.

We had been on the road for about two hours when Don Herndon called. Sam was talking and I was halfway listening and reading a book. All of a sudden Sam got excited and began telling Don things that amazed me. I knew, from the way he was speaking, he had been given a revelation from God. The Lord "spoke" to Sam in a way He had never done before and in so many words said, *"You go back to Mannatech and declare My sovereignty over this company, to the board, to the management, and to the associates, and I'll take care of all the rest. Don't worry about the contracts, the stock, the board, your title, or anything else, I'll take care of all of that."*

I was stunned! I said, "That was definitely a word from the Lord, Sam!" He knew it too and said, "I think we are supposed to go to Orlando right now and give this word to the board members and management who are there and to the field leadership." I agreed, so we turned the car around, went to the airport in Dallas, and headed to Florida.

Sam has often kidded that he only hears from God through me, but this time God clearly revealed directly to Sam what the next move was to be. As sure as I was that Sam would not return to the company until everyone he named in his letter to the board was gone, it was apparent that God had revealed a completely different plan to Sam.

Once in Orlando, we met with Don and Lydia, Bill Greenman, and Peter and Anita Robutka to pray. These people have been a huge support to us for many years, and we needed their spiritual input. It was imperative that we all be in agreement as to how to proceed with the word God had given Sam.

Sam first met with the executive team and told them about his road-to-San Antonio experience. He said he would come back under one condition—that he and I could speak freely about our faith at company events. They all just stared at him with confused looks on their faces. Who could blame them? Just a few days ago Sam sent them a laundry list of conditions that had demanded their contracts be voided and that he be given the chairman position, and now he only had this one request. They must have thought he had gone off the deep end but probably realized they were better off with him than without him.

Sam next met with the Presidential associates and told them his whole story from start to finish. Overall, the response was good. They were glad to have to him back, but some didn't quite understand what had taken place over the last month. They thought that Sam had taken them and the company on a roller coaster ride for nothing. I could understand their frustration because they had a limited knowledge of what we had been dealing with over the years. Sam and I rarely shared with them much of what went on in the company, consequently, they were still in shock over Sam's resignation and now further shocked by his eminent return.

Sam and I then met with Skip and actually had a very good talk. He and I aired out some of our disagreements and apologized for any misunderstandings between us. I then asked if I could pray for him. The meeting was a cleansing of sorts, especially for me. I knew if I was going to be truly effective for God's purposes, then I had to let go of all bitterness and hurt, which with God's grace, I did. Skip also admitted that one of the problems the board had with Sam was his profession of faith. Skip said that the issue would be addressed when Sam met with the board.

The corporate attorney was also in Orlando, and she drew up a contract for Sam to sign. We read it over, but it was worded in a way, which seemed to limit Sam's involvement with MannaRelief. We decided to take some time and make sure that we were doing exactly what God wanted us to do. So we stayed in Orlando and had family time with our children and then went home.

Taking Care Of The Rest

When we returned, one of the board members who had voted Sam out of the company had resigned. This was astounding news! Already the right things were happening without Sam having to do a thing. Sam, however, still had to face the remaining board and give his story.

Right before Sam met with the board, he called me to say he didn't think they were going to agree with his request. We prayed together, and Sam went into the meeting. Once again, he told the story of his "road-to-San Antonio experience" and said he would return on one condition; that he and I be allowed to declare God's sovereignty over the company. They said little to him. No one brought up his previous letters, nor did anyone demand an apology or an explanation.

Sam was asked to leave the room and brought back after a short time. The board had voted to bring him back to the company as a consultant, but felt it was also important that he have some kind of title. They decided on the title of Global Vision Architect. He was also voted back on the Board of Directors and took the place of the individual who had just left. It was as simple as that. We were seeing God's promise in action: *"Declare my sovereignty over the company, and I'll do the rest."* Amazing!

To me it all seemed like a miracle. The warrior spirit in me had been ready for a good fight, but God, in one ten-minute revelation to Sam, had changed the battle strategy to one of grace, humility, and obedience. This was our "ram in the thicket." Only God could use those traits to accomplish His purpose in a situation as hostile as this one had been. What a mighty God we serve!

Sam and I were pleasantly surprised by our alignment with one another. The degree to which we understood and respected each other's gifts and callings was an added blessing. We also recognized the significance of praying together and with the grace of God we've continued to do so. It took a long time to come to this understanding, but I'm overjoyed that we finally did!

During the course of the next few weeks, Sam's attorney and Mannatech's attorney met regularly to discuss the terms of his return and on June 16, 2000, they came to an agreement. In light of recent events, Bob Henry demanded that a contract be drawn up for Sam's consulting services which clearly stated that Sam would have no authority to make any decision on his own, and that he would answer to Bob on every issue. So, for the first time, probably in his entire career, Sam signed a company contract.

Although Sam was now back, and we were comfortable with the terms of his agreement, we knew in our hearts that this was a temporary fix. We believed that God still had some purging and shifting to do in us as well as in the company and that several of the promises He had given us years ago had yet to come to pass.

Decisions were still being made that, in our opinion, lacked integrity or understanding, but Sam knew by faith that God would take care of them all. Sam operated in such freedom now because he no longer carried the burden of the company on his shoulders. He was now following God's lead.

Because of the fiasco of Sam's removal, resignation, and ultimate return, Mannatech's business continued to decline. Some top distributors left, and several who stayed were unsure of the stability of the company. Most people were unaware of the reasons for everything that took place, and some were no longer confident in Sam's commitment to them. The stock continued to tumble, which only added to the shakiness of the times. Sam began to speak at associate meetings around the country to instill a level of solidarity and confidence in the field. At times it seemed to be an uphill battle, but Sam remained resolute. As bad as things seemed, he had a complete peace about the future. He had that peace that surpasses all understanding.[4]

The sell-off of Bill's stock had dropped the price to an all-time low. Skip was anxious to sell his stock too but was afraid to dump anymore into an open market. He negotiated a monthly sale of his stock back to the company. The management asked Sam if he wanted to sell any of his stock, to which he said "no," or if he would consider negotiating a lockup of his stock, for a fee, until the price stabilized. Sam explained that he had given his word to the associates that he would not sell any stock until the price exceeded their buy-in price of eight-dollars-per-share. He further explained that the company did not need to pay him anything in order to ensure his word.

The Lord began to move quickly. On May 25, 2001, Skip Fioretti resigned as Chairman of the Board of Directors. By the end of the year, three of the people listed in Sam's proposal/resignation letter had left the company and their five-year contracts had been renegotiated! Bob Henry was moving all of Skip's people out of management, off the Board of Directors, and replacing them with his people. One of the three executives who left had been a board member, and fortunately was replaced by Ray Robbins. Ray was a great addition to the board because he had been with the company from the beginning, and like Sam, he had the best interest of the associates at heart. He was Sam's choice, not one of Bob's personal picks.

With the chairman seat now available, to most associates Sam was the logical choice to fill that void. However, many on the Board of Directors did not agree. Bob proclaimed that Mannatech needed a chairman who had experience with Wall Street and would in turn increase the value of the stock. Bob then suggested that board member and personal friend, Jules Zimmerman, be elected Chairman of the Board. To many associates/stockholders, this was nonsense. (I agreed with them). They wanted Sam back at the top of the company. They wanted leadership, not Wall Street. After the

[4]Philippians 4:7

last several years of self-serving executives, the associates needed someone they could trust and follow, and, in their opinion, that person was Sam. His leadership style empowered them to achieve great results and he derived satisfaction in their achievements. I believed that Bob was intimidated by the possibility of Sam having any position of authority.

(When Sam returned to Mannatech, the Lord gave me a revelation that Sam would become the Chairman of the Board. From many examples in the Bible, I realized that when God chooses us for a task, it's based on our willingness to follow Him more than on our worldly credentials. According to Hebrews 13:21, the Word says, "He will equip you with everything good, so that you may carry out His will." I knew without a doubt, that Sam was completely able to carry out the role of Chairman. It was a position God had called him to.)

At Bob's request, Sam and I went to New York to visit with Jules Zimmerman to discuss the Chairman position. Jules met us at the hotel and we began our discussion. He explained that as a public company whose stock had dropped to less than two dollars per share, Mannatech needed a chairman who had experience and a relationship with Wall Street, and therefore, he would be the best choice for that position. Sam countered that if the company's declining sales were not turned around, Wall Street would not care who was Chairman of the Board. Sam then went on to say that because of his knowledge of the business and his relationship with the associates, he was the most capable person to serve as chairman. Jules argued that since Sam did not have the CEO experience of a large, public company, his being the chairman would greatly inhibit Mannatech's ability to ever boost its stock price.

At that point, I had heard enough of what the "worlds" view of Sam would be and gave my perspective on the issue. I told Jules how the Lord had birthed the company as a result of prayer and that I believed God had chosen and equipped Sam for the position. I then shared with Jules the story of Moses. I told him that Moses felt completely inadequate for the call of God on his life and how he protested against leading the children of Israel out of Egypt. But, God was not interested in Moses' worldly abilities; he was interested in his heart and his willingness to obey. Because Moses trusted in the Lord, he was used mightily to change the course of history.

Jules was astounded and frustrated by my rational. He responded by saying, "Moses was never CFO of Avon, nor did he have the financial experience that I've had." I sat there in disbelief! In retrospect, we were in disbelief of each other. Jules looked me square in the eye and said, "Linda, I will bet you a dinner at any restaurant in the world, that if I am elected Chairman, our stock will be trading at over six dollars per share by this time next year." I responded by saying, "Jules, if Sam is not elected Chairman, our stock will drop to less than one dollar by this time next year." By now, I knew God was going to confound the wisdom of the "wise." I had no doubt whatsoever that Mannatech would not be on track with its destiny until Sam was in his rightful place of authority.

Sam thanked everyone for their honesty and passion and agreed that we would pray about it and let Jules know what our decision would be. We then went to dinner together and had a nice evening talking about our families and non-business related issues.

I believe that Jules Zimmerman is a good person and that he definitely brought needed experience to the Board of Directors. However, he, like many others, never grasped the greater vision and destiny of the Lord on this Joseph Company.

The annual shareholders meeting was just around the corner, and the heat was on to make a decision about the chairman position. Several associates/shareholders launched a huge campaign to communicate their view, but the board continued to defend its position. There were three board members nominated by the company for re-election, but with the help of Lory Davis (who not only is an associate/shareholder, but also an attorney) the associates nominated their own slate of directors. They were very determined in their attempt to be heard and to make the changes they felt were necessary to move the company forward. In an attempt to calm this uprising, the board decided to nominate Sam and Jules as "co-chairman". Unfortunately, this move was too little, too late.

The Vote That Spoke Volumes

June 5, 2001, was a day to remember. About 200 people showed up for our annual shareholders meeting. Many of them came with proxy votes in their hands from people who were unable to attend the meeting. There was a question-and-answer session in which the shareholders could ask anything pertaining to the company. They took full advantage of this time to voice their frustrations and concerns and to get some commitments from the board. Finally, the time came to vote for the two slates of nominees to the board.

There were a total of 24 million shares; so in order to win, a slate had to receive approximately 12 million votes. Sam and I had decided to vote with the slate that the associates put together instead of the company slate. After all, their slate represented the wishes of our stockholders. At the meeting, nearly ten million, on-site and proxy votes, were cast for the shareholders slate, which included Dr. Reg McDaniel, Don Partridge, and Steve Lemme.

The agency hired to count the on-site/proxy votes said they had never seen so many people in attendance at a shareholders meeting independently voting such a large of percentage of stock. Approximately forty percent of the company's stockholders votes were cast at the meeting. The board was obviously very surprised when they found out that Sam had voted against the company slate, but I was glad he had supported the associates.

Although the shareholders slate lost, their efforts made a tremendous impact. That meeting proved that Mannatech has a group of strong, independent, and passionate associates who are willing to go to any lengths to protect their company and to have their voices heard. These associates had proven that they were no longer innocent bystanders in the company, they were an ownership group who would make their voices heard. Things would never be the same again.

Sam and I knew that the position of co-chairman still left him without final authority, but with the momentum that our associates/stock holders had created, we could feel the tide turning. Oh, and by the way, one year later, our stock was less than one dollar per share. Neither Sam nor I were concerned about it because we knew it was confirmation that God still had some work to do.

Chapter Fifteen

Watch And Be
Utterly Amazed

Within one month after the annual shareholders meeting, Skip Fioretti resigned from the Board of Directors of Mannatech. I believe God used the shareholders meeting to show Skip and the board how determined the associates were to make changes. To his credit, Skip made the right decision. All I could think of was how little Sam had done throughout the process. He didn't have to force an agenda, argue or fight for anything. He simply obeyed God's instruction and the rest fell into place.

Even though the company continued buying Skip's stock back from him, he was now, more than ever, on the lookout for an independent buyer. Sam brought a couple of prospective buyers to the table, but nothing worked out. It was obvious Bob was not interested in any buyer that Sam brought to the table. But Sam stood on God's promise to take care of everything. Then one day Bob Henry told Sam that he had met someone at a DSA (Direct Selling Association) meeting who had shown an interest in purchasing Skip's shares. His name was Stan Fredrick. Not only was Stan from Dallas (which was convenient), he had also spent his entire professional life in the direct sales industry and was past chairman of the DSA. Bob arranged a meeting for Sam to meet Stan.

When Sam came home that night after meeting Stan for the first time, he was more excited than I had seen him in a long time. He said he wanted me to meet Stan and his wife Judy. I was thankful Sam initiated that meeting because it showed how far we had come in honoring each other. It was important for Sam to get my perspective on Stan Fredrick.

We met the Fredricks for dinner, and from the moment we sat down, I had tremendous peace. Stan and Judy were so gracious and warm. Throughout dinner we discussed what a great company Mannatech was, but we also told them about some of the challenges we'd faced. Sam also conveyed to Stan how committed the associate leaders had been through all the turmoil. Stan seemed genuinely excited about the future of the company.

On the way home that night Sam and I talked enthusiastically about the fact that our prayers and the prayers of so many others had finally been answered. We both felt very comfortable with Stan and the role he would play in Mannatech. How refreshing it would be to have someone with Stan's experience and character. Sam looked forward to the possibilities that lay ahead with his new partner.

In August 2001, the purchase of Skip's shares was completed, and Stan Fredrick was announced as a new major stockholder in Mannatech. Stan was also given a seat on the Board of Directors, (filling the seat vacated by Skip). For the first time in almost eight years, I could see that the spiritual tide of Mannatech had completely turned. Out of our obedience, God was continuing to do what He had promised Sam—take care of everything. By now, Bill Fioretti had sold almost all of his stock, and Skip had sold most of his and optioned the remainder to Stan. Now the three largest shareholders, Sam, Stan, and Ray Robbins represented the largest interest in the company and were in alignment with God's purpose for Mannatech.

This would be the foundation that would usher in the remaining changes. God had accomplished much, but there was much more to do. Sam was still co-chairman of Mannatech, and even though he had no official position of authority within the company, I knew God was not through. Sam was totally at peace with this role because he believed God's promise to make everything right. He respected Bob's position as CEO and appreciated much of what he had done to clean up the previous mess within the company. I acknowledged that Bob had accomplished some good things, but I knew the Lord would eventually give Sam full authority. Again, on the outside, this seemed unlikely. Mannatech had a Board of Directors which fully supported Bob Henry in his position and I felt that Sam was becoming too complacent. Once again, I prayed for God to intervene. He gave me an early Christmas present as His answer.

Two Fathers of The Faith

In early December 2001 Sam and I were invited by Mannatech associates, Mike and Pam Graddy, to come to Tulsa to meet with Lindsay Roberts, the wife of Richard Roberts and daughter-in-law of Oral Roberts. Mike and Pam are a precious couple who hoped this introduction would bear fruit for all the parties involved. It would turn out to be a very divine appointment.

A few days before we were to leave, I broke a small bone in my foot. However, because of the location of the break, the only thing I could do was wrap it and use a cane or crutches. It was very swollen and I was in quite a bit of pain, but I was determined not to miss this meeting.

Sam and I took an early flight Monday morning and were scheduled to meet with Lindsay Roberts for one hour. We talked to her about our "Joseph Company" and our vision for MannaRelief. I felt very at ease with Lindsay and we spent much longer talking than we had expected. Towards the end of our time together she said that her father-in-law, Oral Roberts, was visiting the campus that day, and asked if we would like to meet him. Of course, we said yes and she took us to his office.

The minute we met him, I felt such humility and graciousness that I have rarely felt on anyone before. He made us feel like our time with him was more important than anything else. Mr. Roberts asked me why my foot was bandaged and I told him that I had broken it. He then prayed for my foot to be healed and it was! Instantly! (God can heal in any way He desires. In my case it was supernatural. However, God designed our body to heal itself and I believe He gave us Mannatech products to assist in that effort. I have seen and heard many testimonials which confirm that.) He then prayed for MannaRelief and for God's protection on it.

After our time with Oral Roberts, we returned to Lindsay's office and she then invited another staff member in to pray for us before we left. He was a tall, elderly, gentleman with a very sweet spirit. Once we were introduced, we briefly told him about MannaRelief and Mannatech.

Sam said he wanted prayer to stop any plan of the enemy (spiritually speaking) that would use government agencies or those in the health care industry against Mannatech. The man walked behind Sam and put his hands on Sam's shoulders. He said that God showed him that our immediate concern was actually internal. He said the Lord showed him a high ranking executive in Mannatech whose vision was not in line with God's plan for our company. He then proceeded to describe, in detail, what this executive looked like. Sam and I looked at each other in disbelief. He had described our CEO, Bob Henry, in exact detail. (It's very important that you understand that neither the staff member nor I believe that Bob Henry was or is an evil man. God was simply giving us important information about Bob and his relationship to Mannatech.)

The staff member had never met us before nor had he ever heard of Mannatech, but God used him to speak directly into Sam's heart and I think that for the first time, Sam saw Bob through spiritual eyes. He saw that Bob's agenda truly was different than his own. All I could say was, "Thank you Lord for how you answer our prayers. Thank you Lord for how you steer us in the right direction. Thank you Lord for how you protect us." I stand in awe of how incredibly merciful God is to us all.

As we were saying our goodbyes to the group, Lindsay said that during the prayer time she felt I should write a book about our experiences. I told her that I had never written anything before, but I would pray about it and be obedient to whatever God wanted me to do. Sam said that he, too, had thought the exact thing just moments earlier! I took that to be conformation and soon after began reviewing my journal entries to begin the writing of this book.

What an amazing day! It was such a revealing and strategic time for Sam. Now God could use him in the total restoration process which was about to begin.

Prophetic Confirmation

Just a few weeks after the Tulsa meeting, our friend James Goll came to Dallas. God has anointed James with a prophetic gift and he had many times previously prophesied very accurately into our lives. The Lord has used these prophetic words to encourage our faith. (The Bible is very clear on the gift of prophecy. Acts 2:12 states, *"I will pour out my Spirit upon all people. Your sons and daughters will prophesy, your young men will see visions, and your old men will dream dreams. In these days I will pour out my Spirit upon all my servants, men and women alike, and they will prophesy."* First Thessalonians 5:20 & 21 says, *"Do not scoff at prophecies, but test everything that is said. Hold on to what is good."*)

James met with our prayer group and prayed with us about Mannatech. As James prayed for me and Sam he very specifically said that God wanted us to be encouraged and patient. He said that even if it took eighteen months, the Lord would remove people and situations that were obstacles to His purpose and He would put Sam in his rightful place of authority. James said that things would look worse before they got better, but not to lose hope. He also said that the Lord was going to bring us another product which would be a combination of our key ingredient (Ambrotose) and something new and that this new product would take Mannatech a quantum leap forward.

On March 5, 2002, God's promise to Sam began to unfold. With Stan Fredrick and Ray Robbins support, Sam was elected Chairman of the Board. It went unnoticed by almost everyone that the month Sam was removed as President of Mannatech, March 2001, the company lost money for the first time in its history. It continued to lose money every single month until March of 2002, the month that Sam was elected Chairman and has remained profitable ever since. Conventional wisdom would say that was coincidental, but in my opinion, it was proof of the favor of God on Sam for the leadership of Mannatech. That was the point I tried to convey to Jules Zimmerman and the Board of Directors when discussing the Chairman position the year before.

Now that Sam was Chairman of the Board, things really started moving. At the next annual shareholders meeting, the Board began to change and over the next two years Mannatech rebuilt its Board with individuals who had extensive experience in the Direct Sales industry. God continued to move in astonishing ways and His blessings began to pour forth.

A Surprise Return—By Special Delivery

With the demand for our core technology growing by leaps and bounds, Dr. McAnalley explained to Sam that in order to meet future demands and to ultimately create a better Ambrotose with better value for our customers, Mannatech would have to invest in the resources needed to create chemical assays for each individual sugar. This would allow us to look at plants from any place on earth and determine its sugar profile. Dr. McAnalley said it might take several years to develop the science needed and was frustrated by the fact that the company had not started the process years before. But the focus of the previous management team had not been supportive of the science department, creating too much turmoil to move forward on such a proposal.

The first step in launching this initiative was to find a chemist with a background in carbohydrate chemistry. Bill said this was critical and might take some time. A few weeks later, Dr. McAnalley got a surprise visit from an old friend from Nigeria, Dr. Alexis Eberendu, the man who had unlocked the structure of the aloe molecule for Bill years before. Alexis told Bill that he was considering moving back to America, but would need a job before doing so. Alexis' experience in carbohydrate technology and his previous work with the aloe molecule would alone have been a tremendous answer to prayer, but the real confirmation that God had shown up again, came next.

Alexis expressed to Bill, his frustration with the lack of resources in Nigeria for finding long term quality projects and as a result, this forced him to work on side projects in his lab. When Dr. McAnalley asked him what he was working on, Alexis responded by saying that he had been developing chemical assays for measuring sugars other than the aloe sugar. Amazing! Alexis was hired on the spot and his work on other sugars allowed Bill to immediately begin working on a better Ambrotose with better economic value. I was reminded of a scripture the Lord had led me to earlier; *"Watch and be astounded at what I will do! For I am doing something in your day, something you wouldn't believe even if someone told you about it."* Habakkuk 1:5 (New Living).

No driving rain storm this time and no UPS driver, but definitely another special delivery of God's provision. It is remarkable to think of how God orchestrated the life of Alexis Eberendu, from assisting Dr. McAnalley in the 1980's, to inspiring him to work in Nigeria on exactly what Mannatech would need some twenty years later, to delivering it at exactly the right time.

Time For Alignment

Sam's return to Mannatech had opened many spiritual doors for God's purposes to be fulfilled. His election to Chairman of the Board began the restoration process for correct alignment. However, in my estimation, there was still one critical position of authority which needed to be addressed; the position of CEO.

The CEO in a public company does have final decision making authority on day to day operational issues and a huge influence on the corporate culture. By outward appearances Bob was a good CEO. He had made some very critical personnel changes and tough financial adjustments. He functioned in his role in a much more productive way than Skip Fioretti had. But spiritually, Bob's thinking was not in line with the destiny on Mannateh. A good example of this was when Bob said he felt the compensation plan was too generous and that Sam had given associates too much influence in the decision making process. Sam's vision, on the other hand, has always been to bless the associates as much as possible for their good work and to let them speak into the company.

During Mannafest in March of 2001, the opening night was to feature Bob, Sam, and Terry Persinger. It was Bob's first big event and he chose to open it with a speech that lasted about an hour and a half, thirty minutes longer than the time allotted. When it came time for Sam to close, there was less than ten minutes left. Key associates were upset with Bob and I sensed that once again Sam was subtly being pushed out of the way.

Sam and I prayed that night that Bob's thinking would change. Sam was hoping Bob would come on board with the Lord's agenda, but spiritually I did not see it happening. I simply felt Bob could not understand the blessing of God on this company.

The Golden Calf

The Vice President of Marketing reported directly to Bob. The business had dropped significantly during last few years of unrest and even though it had turned around, it was a slow recovery. Bob and the marketing V.P. determined that the reason the business was not booming was because our associates were focused on the products instead of the business. During a marketing meeting they expressed the need to turn the focus of Mannatech away from our products. Other companies had been successful selling the business opportunity of network marketing and Mannatech was failing to follow that "proven" strategy. The marketing V.P. announced that a branding project would be necessary in order to give us a "professional" image and that we should move away from our product driven culture.

This branding included changing our look. They wanted to do away with the scripted "M" in our name and change it to block letters. They thought this would give us a more high tech, polished look. Sam was in shock! It was not so much a new look that bothered Sam. What was troubling was the idea that Bob and the V.P. believed a new look would impact sales in a dramatic way. The fact that they believed they could shift Mannatech's culture from product to business was incomprehensible.

From the day I heard of the branding idea, I did not like it. There was a familiarity to this move, which deeply disturbed me. I could not believe they wanted to make these kinds of changes, especially without input from Sam. I felt that changing our look was a huge mistake in many ways, one of them being financial. Everything with our name on it would have to be changed, including our building. But more importantly, they were on the verge of taking the company in a completely different direction. I took comfort in the knowledge that none of these issues were too big for God to handle. I knew that He had not brought us this far to let it all be taken away again.

I sensed there was a far greater issue at hand. God had created this company to bring healing to the nations, but the management team had no vision for that and I felt this move would take Mannatech off course of its' destiny. I was reminded of the story of the golden calf, which is told in Exodus 32. The children of Israel could not see God's vision or purpose for them because they thought they had all the answers. They could not imagine that God's way could be better than theirs, so they made some decisions which had grave consequences. At least now I had direction in how to pray.

Sam pleaded with them to examine the fact that the strength of our business was the combination of our products, the patents and the life changing experiences of product users. The financial opportunity was the by-product of the blessing. But, they could not hear it.

A New Technology

Despite the conflicting visions, the business was moving forward. God was putting things into proper place. Sam was working hard to provide support for Bill McAnalley's new antioxidant product. There was not much support for the project from Bob or the marketing department. They argued for months that the product was long overdue, that Bill had wasted too much time and money, and that this product would never get to market. Sam argued that the project had taken so long because Dr. McAnalley kept finding ways to improve it. Sam was completely optimistic about Bill McAnalleys ability to develop the world's best antioxidant and he believed this product would be a missing link in Mannatechs mission for optimal health. He said antioxidants have long been touted as a necessity to combat today's environment and that almost every degenerative disease is either triggered or exacerbated by free radical damage, which anti-oxidants help combat. Sam knew that Dr. McAnalley was developing an antioxidant product that would go far beyond anything that had ever been formulated before.

Without knowing anything about the science behind the product, I felt that it was going to be the one that James Goll had prophesied about in December of 2001. James had stated that the Lord was going to give Mannatech another product that would take us a quantum leap from where we are now. My feelings were confirmed when Sam came home one night and shared the following story.

From Africans to Aborigines—God Had it Covered

In developing the antioxidant formula, Dr. McAnalley told Sam that he needed the best natural source of vitamin C complex he could find. He said that in researching the world wide data base on vitamin C, the plant that showed the highest level of C complex was a bush plum that grew wild in the northwest region of Australia. However, there were two potential problems. First, the plum had never been cultivated and commercialized. Second, the land where the plum grew was owned by the Aborigines.

Sam said Dr. McAnalley was thrilled with the challenge of overcoming these two obstacles. He said they provided an amazing opportunity to do something no one had ever done before -complete the antioxidant formula with the best C complex of any plant on earth. Bill believed that God had dropped this right into our laps.

Bill McAnalley and Eileen Venum wanted to go immediately to Australia to negotiate with the Aborigine tribe who owned the land and try to get government funding to help set up a plant to process the plums. Sam told them to go, even though he knew it would stir up a hornets nest with those who wanted this project abandoned.

Bill and Eileen were completely successful. They met with the leaders of the Aborigine tribe and discovered that the wild plum was sacred to their people. Its harvest was so important that it was featured on their ancient calendar as a key plant in their culture. The tribal leaders wanted to know why Dr. McAnalley was interested in their sacred plum and what he planned to do with it. Bill and Eileen told them the story of the aloe vera plant and how Bill had been blessed with the discovery of stabilizing its active ingredient. They told how we were now impacting the lives of people all over the world and that we were called to the stewardship of this life changing product. They promised to do the same with the plum. This was not the normal high powered, let's broker a great deal with the Aborigines, type of negotiation. It was the "let's honor what God had made available to one of the worlds oldest cultures and find a way to share it with the world," type of negotiation.

An Australian company called Caradji arranged funding with the government to build a plant to process the plums on sight and filed a patent on the process that stabilized the plums C complex. Bill and Eileen came home with an exclusive on that product. The first batch of stabilized Bush Plum was processed, sent over, and blended into Dr. McAnalley's antioxidant blend. When tested in the lab, it was almost three times more potent than the best of over ninety antioxidant products sold in health food stores, pharmacies, and other direct sales companies.

The most amazing thing to me however, was the fact that the science showed it worked best when combined with Ambrotose. This was the fulfillment of the prophetic word that James Goll gave us; "[Your] next product will be combined with Ambrotose and will take you a quantum leap forward." This new product, Ambrotose AO, was officially launched in the United States and Canada in September 2003 and quickly became an essential product in the goal for global health. Once again, God had come through on His promise.

The antioxidant project was another eye opener for Sam. He realized again that Bob was not in alignment with where Mannatech was destined to go. Mannatech was never going to be "business as usual." Negotiating with Aborigine tribal leaders using Dr. McAnalley's insight and Sam's persistence, instead of bottom line oriented finances, would probably not have occurred to most business executives. God has used this company in the past to confound the wise and I believe He will continue to do so.

Restoration Completed

From my first reaction to the hiring of Bob, I knew he was not meant to oversee the long term future of Mannatech. He had made some important contributions to the company, but it was time for the next phase of Mannatech to begin. I felt God telling me that the floodgates would be opened for Mannatech once it was in full alliance with His purpose.

Sam also acknowledged that a change was now necessary, but he felt there were two challenges to overcome. First, in light of our recent success, it was unlikely that board members would see the need to change the CEO. And second, even if they did, who would they get to replace Bob? I told Sam that I felt God had called him to that position and because of our prayers He had already made a way for that to happen. Sam was reluctant to pursue the CEO position because he was not sure he would be perceived as being qualified for that role. I reminded Sam of the stories of Moses and David which show how God chooses men based on their willingness to serve Him more than their worldly credentials.

We committed it to prayer and waited on the Lord. Sam and I thought of the other part of James Goll's prophetic word; "God will put you in your rightful place of authority, even if it takes eighteen months." That date would be no later than June 2003, a date that coincided with Mannatech's annual shareholders meeting. I did not think this was coincidental. I thought it was exactly God's timing.

In January 2003, the company met with its Presidential Directors in Hawaii. During an open meeting, Brenda Howard, a Presidential Director from Lubbock, Texas, asked the management group why associate leaders had not been consulted on the company logo change, which had taken place during a re-branding project initiated by the marketing department several months earlier. Brenda is the sweetest person you will ever meet, but you could tell she was very passionate about this issue. Sam answered the question by admitting the company had made a mistake by not including the associates in a decision of this magnitude. However, Bob did not agree with Sam.

Bob felt that associates had too much input into company decisions. He was clearly agitated and said, "I'm sorry, but I must speak up on this issue." He proceeded to proclaim that the leadership had indeed been informed of the change through the Associate Council, an elected group of ten leaders who interact with the company on a regular basis on many issues. Bob was upset that management was being accused by associates of any wrong doing.

The last day of the event ended with an Associate Council/

Management meeting. Bob opened with a speech on teamwork and said that the Council and Management should always speak as one voice and that council members should not publicly disagree with management. Sam immediately and calmly voiced his disagreement with Bob's statement and defended the associates' rights to share their opinions. Their two visions were clearly different.

By the time we left Hawaii, many leaders came to me privately and voiced their uneasiness with the things that had transpired. I know that several of these same leaders also took their concerns to Sam and other Board members. Bob was an experienced businessman who had been trained by some of corporate America's best. But, Mannatech has a much higher calling on it than mere business, and therefore those in authority over it must put aside agendas outside its calling.

Sam, Stan, and Ray met back in Dallas to discuss the management challenges which had occurred over the past year. It was clear to all three that Bob and Sam would have a hard time coexisting in the same company. Their styles, vision, and strategies were diametrically opposed. The company needed one leader and Stan and Ray knew that Sam was the obvious choice. In April of 2003, Sam, Stan and Ray met with Bob to discuss their feelings. The outcome of this meeting resulted with Bob's decision to resign. We prayed that God would use the entire Mannatech experience to impact Bob's life in a positive way.

Chapter 16

The Floodgates Open

In May 2003, seventeen months after James Goll's prophetic word, the Board of Directors accepted Bob Henry's resignation and unanimously elected Sam as the new CEO. What seemed absolutely impossible in April of 2000 had come to pass. God had orchestrated the most amazing chain of events that could have possibly occurred. The Lord, determined that His perfect will for Mannatech would be established, opened the spiritual floodgates and began to pour out his blessings in many ways.

- **Blessing Shareholders**

Momentum in the business picked up almost immediately. The stock price went from around two dollars per share to twelve dollars per share by the end of 2003 and Mannatech posted the best year of its ten year history with a thirty-five percent, fifty million dollar increase over 2002. The first quarter of 2004 posted record breaking sales of $58 million, and that record was immediately broken in the second quarter by sales of over $74 million!

- **Blessing Children**

Also in 2003, MannaRelief completed a retrospective survey project on over one hundred children with Cystic Fibrosis, the number one genetic killer of children in North America. The survey tracked quality of life improvements in their respiratory and/or digestive abilities while using glyconutritional products. Over eighty percent of the children showed improvement in one or both categories. This statistic is staggering in a condition which typically gets progressively worse. From experience we have seen that these types of results absolutely baffle organizations that have a financial stake in the sickness industry. But we continue to press forward because the rewards are so great. Words cannot express the feeling I have, knowing that the quality of life for these children was so positively impacted.

Products for many of these children were funded by a grant received from the Teammates for Kids Foundation, which was started and funded by Garth Brooks. The remaining products were funded by donations from Mannatechs management and associates. It was such a blessing to see how many people from all areas of the company gave so generously.

- **Blessing Women**

In June of 2003, as I was praying, the Lord told me that He wanted me to host ladies conferences. I had no idea how that was going to take place, but I told the Lord I was willing as long as He equipped me. Not long after this time, Sam and I had dinner with

Neecie Moore and her husband Gary Watson. Neecie had been a long time friend and Gary had been the first General Counsel of Mannatech. When Gary left Mannatech we lost touch with them, so we were very happy to rekindle our friendship. Towards the end of dinner, Neecie said that the Lord told her she was going to do women's conferences and she believed she was to do them with me. I was amazed at what I heard! If I had any doubt that the Lord had spoken to me about this, I no longer did.

I am so thankful that the Lord reconnected me with Neecie. She has tremendous experience in many areas that pertain to women. She is also a psychologist and a wonderful woman of God. I was excited to see what God was going to orchestrate in this partnership.

I began praying more specifically about the conferences. During that time the word "renew" came into my mind, but I had no idea what it meant. Later in the week, Sam and I had dinner with Neecie and Gary again and I told them about the word renew. Neecie told me that she prayed about a name for the conferences and the Lord told her to call them "MannaRenew." Once again, I was amazed at the way God cares about every area of our lives and how He will often times confirm His word.

The first thing Neecie and I did was put together a prayer team with Lydia Herndon as the head of it. We both knew that in order for MannaRenew to be successful, the foundation had to be prayer. We made a commitment to pray together, weekly for the events. We prayed for the Lord to direct every aspect of the meetings, from location, to music, to speakers. Neecie, Lydia, and I did not want MannaRenew to reflect who we are, but who God is.

The Mannatech incentive trip in 2003 was in Cancun, Mexico, so we decided to have our first event there. About four hundred women showed up and so did God. It was such a blessing to minister to and pray for so many women. There is something so rewarding about women coming together to share and encourage one another. The reports we got back confirmed that most women were as blessed as we were to be a part of it. Many women said that their lives were truly transformed and they had a renewed hope and vision for themselves and their families.

Our next event was in Dallas in February of 2004 and again the Lord's presence was very powerful. I am so glad that I can be involved with such a wonderful ministry to women. It is exciting to look back and to see how God's plan for Mannatech expanded to the orphans and children of the world and now to women. I can't wait to see what is next.

- **Blessing Mannatechers!**
  God has always brought the right person along side Mannatech at the right time. He must have known that we would need a few more men with impeccable credentials to help validate the potential of glyconutrient technology to even more people. But we could have never conceived who He sent to us this time.

Doctors of Vision

Many doctors have seen and acknowledged the benefits of glyconutrients. Dr. Alex Omelchuk, former Chief of Staff at the Royal Alexandra Hospital in Edmonton, Canada is one such physician. Dr. Omelchuk, was the victim of a massive aneurysm in 1987. Only ten percent of the people survive this kind of stroke. His brain capacity was reduced by thirty percent and he was no longer able to teach or practice medicine. He was told by physicians that he should accept his condition and that he would have to be on pain medicine for the rest of his life.

Over a decade later Dr. Omelchuk was told about glyconutrients and after reading everything he could about them, he decided to try them. Four months after he began the products his quality of life dramatically improved and his thinking became clear. Dr. Omelchuk believes that there is a direct relationship between the regeneration of his brain cells and the products he used. He credits these products with giving him his life back and now travels the world giving lectures on the exciting technology of glyconutrients and introducing thousands of people to their benefits.

In 2004 Dr. John Rollins, former professor of microbiology at Howard University Medical school, retired from the US Patent and Trademark office. His roll as manger of the division that reviewed bio-effective compounds and compositions exposed him to many of the best nutrition and pharmaceutical discoveries of the last 20 years. In a recent interview Dr. Rollins stated that the most significant discovery he had seen in all of his years at the Patent office that might make the biggest impact on the future of health care is the discovery of glyconutrients. Dr. Rollins and his wife Ada are strong Christians and now spend much of their time telling others about glyconutrients.

But perhaps our most prominent voice in the medical community is that of Dr. Benjamin Carson, the director of pediatric neuro surgery at Johns Hopkins University in Baltimore. Time Magazine and CNN named him as one of the top twenty doctors in the United States. In 1987 he was the lead surgeon in the operation that separated the Binder Siamese twins from Germany. It was the first such operation in which both twins survived.

In 2002 Dr. Carson discovered that he had the most aggressive form of prostate cancer. He said that his odds of surviving through traditional medicine alone were not favorable, so he decided to explore a complimentary approach utilizing nutrition. The father of one of Dr.Carson's patients suggested that he call Dr. Reg McDaniel to discuss the use of glyconutrients. After several hours of dialog, Dr. Carson decided to try the products himself. His success of combining these products with standard medical care was far better than he ever expected. He maintained a great quality of life during his treatments and recovered in half the anticipated time.

When Dr. McDaniel heard him speak at the medical symposium, Dr. Carson boldly announced his new secret weapon in dealing with cancer – the complimentary intervention of Ambrotose. Reg said he almost fell out of his chair. He had never known of a doctor with the courage to make such a bold proclamation in front of an audience of fellow doctors, especially oncologists.

Reg told Sam that Dr. Carson's speech was one of the best he had ever heard. He encouraged Sam to do whatever he could to get Dr. Carson to speak at Mannafest, our international event. Sam followed up and personally called him. Dr. Carson said he would be thrilled to speak, but he wanted one hundred percent of his speakers' fee to be sent to his foundation for underprivileged children.

At Mannafest, Dr. Carson came with his administrative assistant, Audrey Jones. When I met her, I knew God had sent us another gift. She and I connected immediately through our common love for the Lord. I pray for her often and hold her dear in my heart. Then I met Dr. Carson. We talked for about twenty minutes and our entire conversation was about God and what great things He had done in our lives. Dr. Carson was such a sincere, humble man and I was honored to spend time with him.

He then went on stage and gave an hour and a half of the most powerful testimony that I have ever heard. He was bold in his positions of societal problems and even bolder in his proclamation of faith. Dr. Carson challenged us in many different areas and kept all six thousand people totally engaged for the entire time. When he finished, the crowd went wild. His stature in the world of medicine and his endorsement of the science of complex sugars was an incredible boost to our associates, who have had to endure the unbelief of those in the health care industry who are ignorant of the science of glycobiology. I'm amazed and grateful that God is inspiring such accomplished individuals to champion the technology that we have been blessed to steward.

Trusting God Pays Big Dividends

By the end of 2003, Mannatech had done so well that the Board of Directors voted to pay its first dividend as a public company. The dividend was announced at ten cents per share. Sam and I are the largest stockholders in Mannatech and stood to earn several hundred thousand dollars from the distribution. We decided to pray about what to do with the money and in a few days Sam said he felt that God had given him an answer. He said that God had blessed us with a company of provision and a technology that has impacted the lives of orphans all over the world and without our help they had little hope for good health. Therefore, Sam said our stock and all the revenue that is generated from it should be dedicated to Kingdom purposes and not for personal wealth building. I agreed with Sam.

I stated earlier that God's Word says if He can trust you with the small things, He will make you ruler over much. I believe the decision to dedicate all of our dividends to MannaRelief and other supporting ministries will continue to open the floodgates of finances for the provision of MannaRelief. It is heartbreaking to think of all the orphans and ill children who desperately need what we can offer them and Sam and I count it a blessing to help out in any way we can.

Sam has publicly said that someday MannaRelief would become larger than Mannatech. I believe that statement was prophetic and that the provision of MannaRelief will become a global phenomenon. Steve Lemme, during Mannafest 2004, said, "If God be your partner, make your plan big." That basically says it all.

A New Team For Such A Time As This

After Sam became CEO, he and Terry Persinger, Mannatech's President and COO, sat down to discuss which responsibilities he and Sam would handle. Sam knew that marketing and science should be his responsibility. He empowered Dr. McAnalley to reconstruct the Research and Development Department and they both began looking for new opportunities to enhance Mannatechs' core technology.

Sam also made a very strategic move by hiring Steve Lemme as Senior Vice President of Sales. As an associate, Steve had earned the reputation in the field as being one of the most dynamic, motivating, and inspirational speakers and was in full alignment with the destiny of the company. Steve and his wife Susanne were living in Minnesota with their three children, but both felt that since Sam was now fully in charge, they needed to come and support the vision. They made a great sacrifice to leave the place they loved and had raised their children in, but they did not want to miss the call of God on their lives.

Within just a few months of Steve's arrival, the top management within the marketing department resigned and Steve was promoted to Senior Vice President of Sales and Marketing. Jim Anderson, whom Sam had worked with years ago, was hired as Executive Director of Marketing Administration. Finally, Dr. Neecie Moore was hired to facilitate the development of a new associate training program and the oversight of the "Power of Purpose" personal development program. God was answering our prayers by bringing in men and women with the credentials as well as the character to make this an even better company. We know he will continue to as long as we seek Him and His kingdom first.

Chapter Seventeen

Reflections

When I think back to May 2000 and see all that God has done since then, I am completely amazed. In less than two years, every single thing that Sam had asked for in his letter to the board was accomplished. First, when Sam was fired, God had given me the story of Abraham and Isaac. We knew God was asking Sam to trust Him completely. Next, we prayed about the letter to the Board of Directors, outlining Sam's no-compromise demands for his return and in doing so, burning every bridge of possible reconciliation with the old guard. Then, on our trip to San Antonio, God revealed His plan for Sam's return to the company with the promise that He would take care of everything, which He did.

To this day many people still ask why Sam resigned. Now you know. It was the most difficult thing he's ever done, but it was the leap of faith God needed to see. In May of 2000, the future of Mannatech looked as dismal as we could have imagined. But by March of 2004 at our annual Mannafest convention, everything was in place to fulfill its destiny!

Mannafest 2004 was quite a celebration. Mannatech was now ten years old and we had so much to be thankful for. I knew there was something very significant in the number ten, but Eugene Fox, a godly man of faith, from Canada summed it up best. He said that "this was the end of the beginning." I really thought about that statement and all that it implied.

I asked several associates, who were with the company during those difficult years, why they stayed with Mannatech. I was curious as to why they stuck it out despite all the ups and downs. Susan Havener, who has had at least twenty years of networking experience, summed it up best when she said, "I was committed to the vision." I'm convinced that's the strongest asset Mannatech has going for it. The product is wonderful, the financial opportunity is great, but the Bible says, *"Without a vision people perish."*[5] Truly it was the vision that kept us alive.

I thought about the story of Joseph once again and wondered how he must have felt when his brothers threw him into a dark, dry well, or when he was falsely accused and thrown into prison. The Bible doesn't say that Joseph was bitter or angry; but, instead, it states time and again that the Lord was with him. In the end, everything that God promised Joseph came true. God honored him by putting him in a position to give provision to a starving world. I'm sure that Joseph reflected on his life and could see that everything he had gone

---

[5]Proverbs 29:18

through, the good and the bad, led him to his final destination.

Sam and I can certainly relate to Joseph's story, now more than ever. Romans 8:28 tells us, *"And we know that God causes all things to work together for good for those who love God, to those who are called according to His purpose."* That Scripture is so fitting for us and for the Undeniable Destiny on this company.

It had been a decade of growth on a personal as well as a business level. Neither Sam nor I would have the spiritual understanding that we do had we not gone through the difficult times. I can also look back and see that Mannatech is a much more solid company because of all it has endured. I have seen the hand of God move in so many ways and I have been privileged that He allowed me to play a part in His plan for global change.

As I Look To The Future.....

I believe God has only begun with His blessing on this Joseph company and that more technology is on the way. Now that Sam is at the head of the company I believe that God will continue to bring people with a desire to further the cause. I've read many stories which tell of the deterioration of our health in virtually every area of our world and according to these stories there seems to be no sign of relief on the horizon. I refuse to accept that the situation is hopeless. I have personally witnessed thousands of testimonies to the contrary. God will use many ways to bring healing to the world and it makes perfect sense to me that the Creator of our universe would use natural products as one way to accomplish this purpose. I know Mannatech's products are a part of His plan for health and healing.

It is remarkable that God provided a mixture of sugar molecules to support the body's recovery processes in such a dramatic way. But, with billions of dollars being spent on medical research each year, man is determined to "lean on his own understanding" for every answer. Whether that comes from ignorance or pride, the acceptance of this gift has been an uphill battle for some because it has come in a form the "wise" cannot easily accept. First Corinthians 3:19 states, *"For the wisdom of this world is foolishness to God."* I pray that God will begin to open the eyes of those who, until now, have had them shut.

God inspired Sam to use the distribution model of network marketing for Mannatech. Having never been in business, I was surprised at the contempt which is sometimes associated with this industry, especially from within the Christian community. I have no doubt that some people have had negative experiences with other products or companies and that it's caused them to react the way they do. I can certainly relate to them because that's how Sam and I judged the church for years. We were so offended by the arrogance of some Church leaders and the hypocrisy of others, that we turned our hearts away from the Truth. I'm thankful that God was merciful enough to help us through our issues and give us the discernment not to judge all Christians based on the actions of a few.

Many have come to Mannatech because they say God called them to it. When I think back to my dream in the very beginning about being in the football stadium filled with people, I believe God is calling multitudes to join us. And I believe God will use this company to make available the provision of health and finances in ways we have yet to see.

I believe the flood gates are also about to open for MannaRelief as we continue to provide this unique support for the worlds most medically fragile children. MannaRelief expresses the true heart of God for the lost and hurting. Hundreds of volunteers have already joined this ministry to serve the hopeless, and I pray thousands more will join.

I believe that the company's support of MannaRelief will determine Mannatech's ultimate success. I feel certain that if the company ever turns its back on MannaRelief, God will lift His blessing from it. Mannatech's giving to MannaRelief is as strategic to its success as any other component.

My mind cannot fathom what the next ten years will bring, but I will walk this journey a step at a time and fully trust in the Lord to direct me. And, I'll always be thankful.

I'm thankful for all the trials and tribulations I went though because they caused me to trust in God to a greater measure.

I'm thankful that God never turned away from me even though I turned away from Him.

I'm thankful that God continued to teach me, train me and direct me in spite of my ignorance.

I'm thankful for everything Sam and I have been through because it's prepared us for what's ahead. So I look to the future with much anticipation and wonder.

Epilogue

The Road Ahead

This is by no means the end of our journey. As amazing as our story is, I don't think we've even scratched the surface of what God has in store for us. I am more excited now than the day we started Mannatech. Sam and I continue to proclaim God's sovereignty over the company, and God continues to open new doors we didn't even know existed. I know, with all my heart, that if we continue to humble ourselves and edify one another, God will bless the world through this "Joseph Company." He has prepared us and equipped us to perform this task, and we relish the challenge.

David Wilkerson is a pastor who has a publication called "Times Square Church Pulpit Series"and in the December 31, 2001 issue he made some profound observations that I'd like to share with you as they relate to Mannatech being a company of destiny.

"In every generation, the Lord raises up a Joseph Company. He takes these devoted servants through years of trouble and trials, to prove and strengthen their faith. And he delivers them from many satanic snares. But the Joseph Company is tested in ways that few others experience. They face tormenting doubts, pressing fears, fierce temptations. And, perhaps most painfully of all, they're tried by God's Word... How was Joseph tried by God's Word? He knew, all through his sufferings, that he was a righteous man. He knew he had a heart for God. And that only made his trials more baffling... As he looked back over his journey, he realized, 'I see now the Lord was in it all. And that makes everything I suffered, every painful, lonely moment, worth it.' Joseph made peace with his past, because he saw God's hand in it... What an incredible revelation for Joseph. Yet, what's the lesson for God's people today? It is this: our Lord has preserved us in the past. He will preserve us in the days ahead. And most important of all, he has an eternal purpose behind it all."

My Prayer...

I pray that if you've never accepted Jesus Christ into your heart as the true, living God that you'll do so now. If you're struggling with who Jesus is I recommend a book called, "The Case For Christ," by Lee Strobel. It will answer many of the questions you may have about giving your life to Christ.

I pray that if you have received Jesus into your life you will desire to know Him at a deeper level.

I pray that you will see Him not only as an awesome and magnificent God, but as a loving and merciful Father.

I pray that you will see Him as a limitless God who wants to use you in limitless ways.

And lastly, I pray that you will find and embrace your own journey into an Undeniable Destiny.

Bringing
Health
and
Hope
to the
Children
of the
World

MannaRelief

Imagine a Child Who No Longer Dreams...

A child like Monica...

Once her blue eyes danced as she played her clarinet for hours at a time. She would be a great musician some day. Then Monica's small body became racked with constant, piercing pain. "Inoperable brain tumor," the doctors said. Now her fingers are swollen from chemotherapy. Her clarinet lies silent in its case.

Or Billy...

Billy once enjoyed life to the fullest, but recently the diagnosis of chronic asthma has forced him out of the activities he used to share with his friends and classmates. He just joined the ranks of millions who now suffer from a growing number of respiratory conditions.

Or Sorina...

The neighbors found her abandoned in the street. They took her to the orphanage. She was afraid. The room the busy lady put her in was a cold dingy gray, and there weren't any toys. Now Sorina lies on her cot all day with the rows of other silent children, wondering where her Mommy went and when she's coming back.

What if one of these children was yours? And what if your decision to act could help one of them dream again? Now, you can.

Imagine the Joy...

Introducing MannaRelief

Years ago in adopting children of their own, Sam and Linda Caster awakened to a simple realization: they could make a crucial difference in the life of a child. The Caster's lives have never been the same, as they experience the dreams and priceless joy of their children each and every day.

Motivated by their faith that God sees all children as His own, the Casters began a journey to couple their experience of running a multi-million dollar nutritional company with their life-changing love for children—and eventually formed MannaRelief ministries.

Since 1999, MannaRelief has transformed the lives of thousands of children in over 30 countries—distributing millions of dollars worth of nutritional enhancement products through more than 300 life-giving ministries.

Today, MannaRelief proudly offers *Hope, Blessing*, and *Results*.

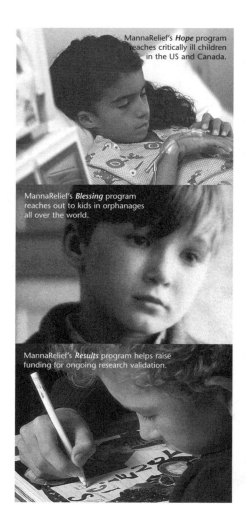

MannaRelief's *Hope* program reaches critically ill children in the US and Canada.

MannaRelief's *Blessing* program reaches out to kids in orphanages all over the world.

MannaRelief's *Results* program helps raise funding for ongoing research validation.

Currently focused in North America, MannaRelief's Hope is a six-month program for medically fragile children and those with other health challenges. Any child with a chronic condition is eligible for sponsorship. Each child may also be renewed by their sponsor for additional 6 month periods. Sponsorship for these children comes from personal, group, corporate, civic, foundation and ecumenical donations.

THE ORPHANS OF THE WORLD

MannaRelief's Blessing is a six-month program that reaches out and nourishes children in orphanages around the globe. Church and civic organizations have joined the ranks of personal and group sponsorship in this effort. MannaRelief also organizes group visits to overseas orphanages for those sponsors who desire to get more involved in the lives of these precious children. The Blessing program is truly an effective way to touch the lives of the world's most fragile children.

RESEARCH THAT MAKES A DIFFERENCE TODAY

For decades, billions of research dollars have been poured into the search for the origin of a growing number of childhood diseases that continue to proliferate our world. MannaRelief's Results program helps fund research to validate the impact we can make on the quality of life of these children today. Finding long term solutions will remain the target of mainstream medicine, but helping to reduce the suffering now is the calling on MannaRelief.

Science That Serves

MannaRelief has boldly raised the standard of accountability for faith-based and charitable organizations by proactively seeking objective expertise to validate the results of our programs.

Medical Oversight

Dr. Reg McDaniel, M.D. provides medical oversight for the Hope Program. Protocols for nutritional support are recommended for each recipient on a case by case basis.

Dr. McDaniel, former Chief of Staff and Chief of Pathology of a Dallas metroplex hospital has done over 20 trials and case studies on the complementary use of standardized dietary supplements.

Research

MannaRelief also raises funding to provide financial support and products for ongoing research projects. These research projects are designed to validate the impact of necessary but often missing micronutrients in the diets of children suffering from a variety of chronic conditions.

Imagine You Being Involved...

As a MannaRelief partner, you can empower a child to dream again. Thanks to people like you who have contributed to MannaRelief, Monica can dare to dream again, Billy can experience a new breath of life, and Sorina now knows how it feels to be nourished, hugged and loved by God.

Be a MannaRelief Hero!

Never thought you'd be a hero? Well, now's your chance. Contribute to one or more of MannaRelief's programs, and you'll become a Hero in a child's eyes. You can sponsor a child through MannaRelief's Hope program, fund research through the Results program or you can bring Blessing to an entire orphanage of your choice. Or you can give Hope, Blessing and Results to children around the world by donating to MannaRelief.

Be a MannaRelief Champion!

Every child needs a champion – some more than others. Volunteer to be a MannaRelief Champion, and become an important advocate and voice for needy children around the world. MannaRelief will count on you to connect children, orphanages, Heroes, and other Champions with its programs.

Three Elements to Each Program

Each of MannaRelief's three wellness programs implement a powerful, three-pronged approach designed to improve the quality of life for suffering children.

Nutrition

MannaRelief provides each child in its programs with a combination of vitamins and minerals, vine-ripened fruit and vegetable extracts, essential amino and fatty acids for basic nutritional support, plant-synthesized adaptagens to support endocrine function and combat stress, and a blend of patent-protected glyconutrients which offer the latest discovery in the support of overall immune function. These nutritional components are all-natural and have a proven track record for increasing the quality of life for children with a wide variety of ailments, from malnutrition to terminal illness. MannaRelief products and their ingredients have been showcased in hundreds of peer-reviewed published papers, many of which can be found at *www.glycoscience.org*.

Attention

Medical research has repeatedly shown that nurturing, personal attention is key to the healthy development of a child. New data also suggests that attention can play a key role in the recovery process. MannaRelief provides this data to the loving parents of medically fragile children, to help validate the practical importance of this component and to encourage them in their long hours of care giving.

Prayer

Recently published clinical trials now validate the Biblical promise of the power of prayer in healing of the sick. The founders, staff and many of the Champions and Heroes of MannaRelief are joined with parents, guardians and friends in ongoing prayer support for every recipient child in each of MannaRelief's programs.

For more information or to commit as a MannaRelief Hero or Champion, visit **www.mannarelief.org**. You may also complete the MannaRelief commitment envelope.

About the Founders

In the eyes of co-founders Sam and Linda Caster, the creation of MannaRelief has been clearly providential. This powerful, life-giving ministry has provided them with a unique opportunity to integrate and maximize their God-given gifts and callings, uniting Linda's prayer gifting and strong desire to honor God with Sam's compassionate nature and ability to create provision. Sam and Linda reside in Dallas, TX with their children.

"We who are strong must bear the infirmities of the weak and not seek to please ourselves."

Romans 15:1

P.O. Box 540669
Grand Prairie, Texas 75054 USA

Phone: 817-557-8700 • Fax: 817-557-8750
E-mail: info@mannarelief.org • **www.mannarelief.org**